Careers in Focus

Performing Arts

Ferguson Publishing Company
Chicago, Illinois

Editorial Staff
Andrew Morkes, *Managing Editor-Career Publications*
Carol Yehling, *Senior Editor*
Anne Paterson, *Editor*
Nora Walsh, *Assistant Editor*

Library of Congress Cataloging-in-Publication Data

Careers in focus. Performing arts.
    p. cm.
Includes index.
Summary: Discusses career possibilities in the performing arts and includes information about the requirements of each job, the necessary preparation, ways to get started, salaries, and the future potential of jobs in this field.
  ISBN 0-89434-431-5 (alk. paper)
  1. Performing arts--Vocational guidance. [1. Performing arts--Vocational guidance. 2. Vocational guidance.]   I. Title: Performing arts. II. Ferguson Publishing Company.
  PN1580 .C36 2002
  791'.023--dc21

                                        2001008734

Printed in the United States of America

Cover photo courtesy Zephyr Picture/Index Stock Imagery

Published and distributed by
Ferguson Publishing Company
200 West Jackson Boulevard, 7th Floor
Chicago, Illinois 60606
800-306-9941
www.fergpubco.com

Z-2

Table of Contents

Introduction

The stereotype of the starving artist—the poor soul who has given up all the conveniences of modern life for the sake of art—still fits a large group of musicians, comedians, actors, and other performers. But for a growing number of creative, talented, highly skilled people, the field of performing arts offers hundreds of fulfilling and quite lucrative job opportunities. The artist no longer has to starve.

Perhaps one of the secrets to making a living as a performing artist is to specialize and carve out a niche for your special talents. Composers, for example, can specialize in advertising jingles, and filmmakers can concentrate only on documentaries. Many successful artists are unable to fit into one niche but are multitalented. A dancer who knows music and stage production is likely to find more work, as is an actor who can also sing and dance. Those who take the time to learn about related arts and industries and develop a variety of skills are likely to find more opportunities.

This book describes a variety of careers in the performing arts, in areas of music, theater, dance, film, and television. These careers are as diverse in nature as they are in their work environments, education requirements, and advancement potential. Earnings vary from as little as $50 for a magician who performs at a child's birthday party to over $1 million for a well-known actor who performs a lead role in a movie.

Some positions require a high school diploma, while others require a college degree. Teachers will need a more advanced degree, such as a master's in fine arts or education. All of the occupations in this book require significant expertise, whether through formal education or work experience.

Traditional vertical advancement is possible—a production assistant can become a film editor and eventually a director. But lateral movement is also common in the arts and entertainment field-a dancer might become an actor and then move into directing. Depending on your particular talents and what you learn through your various work experiences, there is great opportunity to cross over into other areas of the performing arts.

The outlook for entertainment occupations is good. The film and television industries have exploded in recent years with the development of the Internet, cable television, high definition television (HDTV), home movie rentals, and digital recording and processing technology. Managers of resorts, theaters, and concert venues will also continue to need entertainers, booking comedians, magicians, and rock bands to please audiences of all ages. For some occupations, however, the competition is so stiff that it drives earnings to below minimum wage and makes the prime jobs available to only a select few. Actors, writers, and other artists frequently have to find other ways to support themselves.

Each article in *Careers in Focus: Performing Arts* discusses in detail a particular occupation in the performing arts. Many of the articles appear in Ferguson's *Encyclopedia of Careers and Vocational Guidance* but have been updated and revised with the latest information from the U.S. Department of Labor and other sources. The **Overview** section is a brief introductory description of the duties and responsibilities of a person in the career. Oftentimes, a career may have a variety of job titles. When this is the case, alternative career titles are presented in this section. The **History** section describes the history of the particular job as it relates to the overall development of its industry or field. **The Job** describes the primary and secondary duties of the job. **Requirements** discusses high school and postsecondary education and training requirements, any certification or licensing necessary, and any other personal requirements for success in the job. **Exploring** offers suggestions on how to gain some experience in or knowledge of the particular job before making a firm educational and financial commitment. The focus is on what can be done while still in high school (or in the early years of college) to gain a better understanding of the job. The **Employers** section gives an overview of typical places of employment for the job. **Starting Out** discusses the best ways to land that first job, whether through the college placement office, newspaper ads, or personal contact. The **Advancement** section describes what kind of career path to expect from the job and how to get on it. **Earnings** lists salary ranges and describes the typical fringe benefits. The **Work Environment** section describes the typical surroundings and conditions of employment, whether indoors or outdoors, noisy or quiet, social or independent, and so on. Also discussed are typical hours worked, any seasonal fluctuations, and the stresses and strains of the job. The **Outlook** section summarizes the job in terms of the general economy and industry projections. For the most part, Outlook information is obtained from the U.S. Bureau of Labor Statistics and is supplemented by information taken from professional associations. Job growth terms follow those used in the *Occupational Outlook Handbook*. Growth described as "much faster than the average" means an increase of 36 percent or more. Growth described as "faster than the average" means an increase of 21 to 35 percent. Growth described as "about as fast as the average" means an increase of 10 to 20 percent. Growth described as "little change or more slowly than the average" means an increase of 0 to 9 percent. "Decline" means a decrease of 1 percent or more. Each article ends with **For More Information,** which lists organizations that can provide career information on training, education, internships, scholarships, and job placement.

Actors

Overview

Actors play parts or roles in dramatic productions on the stage, in motion pictures, or on television or radio. They impersonate, or portray, characters by speech, gesture, song, and dance. There are approximately 105,000 actors employed in the United States.

History

Drama was refined as an art form by the ancient Greeks, who used the stage as a forum for topical themes and stories. The role of actors became more important than in the past, and settings became more realistic with the use of scenery. Playgoing was often a great celebration, a tradition carried on by the Romans. The rise of the Christian church put an end to theater in the sixth century AD, and for several centuries actors were ostracized from society, surviving as jugglers and jesters.

Drama was reintroduced during the Middles Ages but became more religious in focus. Plays during this period typically centered around biblical themes, and roles were played by priests and other amateurs. This changed with the rediscovery of Greek and Roman plays in the Renaissance. Professional actors and acting troupes toured the countries of Europe, presenting ancient plays or improvising new dramas based on cultural issues and situations of the day. Actors began to take on more prominence in society. In England, actors such as Will Kemp (?-1603?) and Richard Burbage (1567-1619) became known for their roles in the plays of William Shakespeare (1564-1616). In France, Moliere (1622-73) wrote and often acted in his own plays. Until the mid-17th century, however, women were banned from the stage, and the roles of women were played by young boys.

By the 18th century, actors could become quite prominent members of society, and plays were often written—or, in the case of Shakespeare's plays, rewritten—to suit a particular actor. Acting styles tended to be highly exaggerated, with elaborate gestures and artificial speech, until David Garrick (1717-79) introduced a more natural style to the stage in the mid-1700s. The first American acting company was established in Williamsburg, Virginia, in 1752, led by Lewis Hallan. In the next century, many actors became stars: famous actors of the time included Edwin Forrest (1806-72), Fanny (1809-93) and Charles Kemble (1775-1854), Edmund Kean (1787-1833), William Charles Macready (1793-1873), and Joseph Jefferson (1829-1905), who was particularly well known for his comedic roles.

Until the late 19th century, stars dominated the stage. But in 1874, George II, Duke of Saxe-Meiningen, formed a theater troupe in which every actor was given equal prominence. This ensemble style influenced others, such as Andre Antoine of France, and gave rise to a new trend in theater called naturalism, which featured far more realistic characters in more realistic settings than before. This style of theater came to dominate the 20th century. It also called for new methods of acting. Konstantin Stanislavsky (1863-1938) of the Moscow Art Theater, who developed an especially influential acting style that was later called method acting, influenced the Group Theater in the United States; one member, Lee Strasberg (1901-82), founded the Actors Studio in New York, which would become an important training ground for many of the great American actors. In the early 20th century, vaudeville and burlesque shows were extremely popular and became the training ground for some of the great comic actors of the century.

By then, developments such as film, radio, and television offered many more acting opportunities than ever before. Many actors honed their skills on the stage and then entered one of these new media, where they could become known throughout the nation and often throughout the world. Both radio and television offered still more acting opportunities in advertisements. The development of sound in film caused many popular actors from the silent era to fade from view, while giving rise to many others. But almost from the beginning, film stars were known for their outrageous salaries and lavish style of living.

In the United States, New York gradually became the center of theater and remains so, although community theater companies abound throughout the country. Hollywood is the recognized center of the motion picture and television industries. Other major production centers are Miami, Chicago, San Francisco, Dallas, and Houston.

The Job

The imitation or basic development of a character for presentation to an audience often seems like a glamorous and fairly easy job. In reality, it is demanding, tiring work requiring a special talent.

The actor must first find a part available in some upcoming production. This may be in a comedy, drama, musical, or opera. Then, having read and studied the part, the actor must audition before the director and other people who have control of the production. This requirement is often waived for established artists. In film and television, actors must also complete screen tests, which are scenes recorded on film, at times performed with other actors, which are later viewed by the director and producer of the film.

If selected for the part, the actor must spend hundreds of hours in rehearsal and must memorize many lines and cues. This is especially true in live theater; in film and television, actors may spend less time in rehearsal and sometimes improvise their lines before the camera, often performing several attempts, or "takes," before the director is satisfied. Actors on television often take advantage of teleprompters, which scroll their lines on a screen in front of them while performing. Radio actors generally read from a script, and therefore rehearsal times are usually shorter.

In addition to such mechanical duties, the actor must determine the essence of the character being portrayed and the relation of that character to the overall scheme of the play. Radio actors must be especially skilled in expressing character and emotion through voice alone. In many film and theater roles, actors must also sing and dance and spend additional time rehearsing songs and perfecting the choreography. Some roles require actors to perform various stunts, which can be quite dangerous. Most often, these stunts are performed by specially trained *stunt performers*. Others work as *stand-ins* or *body doubles*. These actors are chosen for specific features and appear on film in place of the lead actor; this is often the case in films requiring nude or seminude scenes. Many television programs, such as game shows, also feature *models,* who generally assist the host of the program.

Actors in the theater may perform the same part many times a week for weeks, months, and sometimes years. This allows them to develop the role, but it can also become tedious. Actors in films may spend several weeks involved in a production, which often takes place on location, that is, in different parts of the world. Television actors involved in a series, such as a soap opera or a situation comedy, also may play the same role for years, generally in 13-week cycles. For these actors, however, their lines change from week to week and even from day to day, and much time is spent rehearsing their new lines.

While studying and perfecting their craft, many actors work as *extras,* the nonspeaking characters who appear in the background on screen or stage. Many actors also continue their training. A great deal of an actor's time is spent attending auditions.

Requirements

High School

There are no minimum educational requirements to become an actor. However, at least a high school diploma is recommended.

Postsecondary Training

As acting becomes more and more involved with the various facets of our society, a college degree will become more important to those who hope to have an acting career. It is assumed that the actor who has completed a liberal arts program is more capable of understanding the wide variety of roles that are available. Therefore, it is strongly recommended that aspiring actors complete at least a bachelor's degree program in theater or the dramatic arts. In addition, graduate degrees in the fine arts or in drama are nearly always required should the individual decide to teach dramatic arts.

College can also serve to provide acting experience for the hopeful actor. More than 500 colleges and universities throughout the country offer dramatic arts programs and present theatrical performances. Actors and directors recommend that those interested in acting gain as much experience as possible through acting in plays in high school and college or in those offered by community groups. Training beyond college is recommended, especially for actors interested in entering the theater. Joining acting workshops, such as the Actors Studio, can often be highly competitive.

Other Requirements

Prospective actors will be required not only to have a great talent for acting but also a great determination to succeed in the theater and motion pictures. They must be able to memorize hundreds of lines and should have a good speaking voice. The ability to sing and dance is important for increasing the opportunities for the young actor. Almost all actors, even the biggest stars, are required to audition for a part before they receive the role. In film and television, they will generally complete screen tests to see how they will appear on film. In all fields of acting, a love for acting is a must. It might take many years for an actor to achieve any success, if at all.

Performers on the Broadway stages must be members of the Actors' Equity Association before being cast. While union membership may not always be required, many actors find it advantageous to belong to a union that covers their particular field of performing arts. These organizations include the Actors' Equity Association (stage), Screen Actors Guild or Screen Extras Guild (motion pictures and television films), or American Federation of Television and Radio Artists (TV, recording, and radio). In addition, some actors may benefit from membership in the American Guild of Variety Artists (nightclubs, and so on), American Guild of Musical Artists (opera and ballet), or organizations such as the Hebrew Actors Union or Italian Actors Union for productions in those languages.

Exploring

The best way to explore this career is to participate in school or local theater productions. Even working on the props or lighting crew will provide insight into the field.

Also, attend as many dramatic productions as possible and try to talk with people who either are currently in the theater or have been at one time. They can offer advice to individuals interested in a career in the theater.

Many books, such as *Beginning* (New York: St. Martin's, 1989), by Kenneth Branagh, have been written about acting, not only concerning how to perform but also about the nature of the work, its offerings, advantages, and disadvantages.

Employers

Motion pictures, television, and the stage are the largest fields of employment for actors, with television commercials representing as much as 60 percent of all acting jobs. Most of the opportunities for employment in these fields are either in Los Angeles or in New York. On stage, even the road shows often have their beginning in New York, with the selection of actors conducted there along with rehearsals. However, nearly every city and most communities present local and regional theater productions.

As cable television networks continue to produce more and more of their own programs and films, they will become a major provider of employment for actors. Home video will also continue to create new acting jobs, as will the music video business.

The lowest numbers of actors are employed for stage work. In addition to Broadway shows and regional theater, there are employment opportunities for stage actors in summer stock, at resorts, and on cruise ships.

Starting Out

Probably the best way to enter acting is to start with high school, local, or college productions and to gain as much experience as possible on that level. Very rarely is an inexperienced actor given an opportunity to perform on stage or in film in New York or Hollywood. The field is extremely difficult to enter; the more experience and ability beginners have, however, the greater the possibilities for entrance.

Those venturing to New York or Hollywood are encouraged first to have enough money to support themselves during the long waiting and searching period normally required before a job is found. Most will list themselves with a casting agency that will help them find a part as an extra or a bit player, either in theater or film. These agencies keep names on file along with photographs and a description of the individual's features and experience, and if a part comes along that may be suitable, they contact that person. Very often, however, names are added to their lists only when the number of people in a particular physical category is low. For instance, the agency may not have enough athletic young women on their roster, and if the applicant happens to fit this description, her name is added.

Advancement

New actors will normally start in bit parts and will have only a few lines to speak, if any. The normal procession of advancement would then lead to larger supporting roles and then, in the case of theater, possibly to a role as understudy for one of the main actors. The understudy usually has an opportunity to fill in should the main actor be unable to give a performance. Many film and television actors get their start in commercials or by appearing in government and commercially sponsored public service announcements, films, and programs. Other actors join the afternoon soap operas and continue on to evening programs. Many actors have also gotten their start in on-camera roles such as presenting the weather segment of a local news program. Once an actor has gained experience, he or she may go on to play stronger supporting roles or even leading roles in stage, television, or film productions. From there, an actor may go on to stardom. Only a very small number of actors ever reach that pinnacle, however.

Some actors eventually go into other, related occupations and become drama coaches, drama teachers, producers, stage directors, motion picture directors, television directors, radio directors, stage managers, casting directors, or artist and repertoire managers. Others may combine one or more of these functions while continuing their career as an actor.

Earnings

The wage scale for actors is largely controlled through bargaining agreements reached by various unions in negotiations with producers. These agreements normally control the minimum salaries, hours of work permitted per week, and other conditions of employment. In addition, each artist enters into a separate contract that may provide for higher salaries.

In 2002, the minimum daily salary of any member of the Screen Actors Guild (SAG) in a speaking role was $655, or $2,272 for a five-day workweek. Motion picture actors may also receive additional payments known as residuals as part of their guaranteed salary. Many motion picture actors receive residuals whenever films, TV shows, and TV commercials in which they appear are rerun, sold for TV exhibition, or put on videocassette. Residuals often exceed the actors' original salary and account for about one-third of all actors' income.

A wide range of earnings can be seen when reviewing the Actors' Equity Association's *Annual Report 2000,* which includes a breakdown of average weekly salaries by contract type and location. According to the report, for example, those in "Off Broadway" productions earned an average weekly salary of $642 during the 1999-2000 season. Other average weekly earnings for the same period include: San Francisco Bay area theater, $329; New England area theater, $236; Disney World in Orlando, Florida, $704; and Chicago area theater, $406. The report concludes that the median weekly salary for all contract areas is $457. Most actors do not work 52 weeks per year; in fact, the report notes that of the 38,013 members in good standing only 16,976 were employed. The majority of those employed, approximately 12,000, had annual earnings ranging from $1 to $15,000.

According to the U.S. Department of Labor, the median yearly earnings of all actors was $25,920 in 2000. The department also reported the lowest paid 10 percent earned less than $12,700 annually, while the highest paid 10 percent made more than $93,620.

The annual earnings of persons in television and movies are affected by frequent periods of unemployment. According to SAG, most of its members earn less than $7,500 a year from acting jobs. Unions offer health, welfare, and pension funds for members working over a set number of weeks a year. Some actors are eligible for paid vacation and sick time, depending on the work contract.

In all fields, well-known actors have salary rates above the minimums, and the salaries of the few top stars are many times higher. Actors in television series may earn tens of thousands of dollars per week, while a few may earn as much as $1 million or more per week. Salaries for these actors vary considerably and are negotiated individually. In film, top stars may earn as much as $20 million per film, and, after receiving a percentage of the gross earned by the film, these stars can earn far, far more.

Until recent years, female film stars tended to earn lower salaries than their male counterparts; the emergence of stars such as Demi Moore, Julia Roberts, Jodie Foster, and others has started to reverse that trend. The average annual earnings for all motion picture actors, however, are usually low for all but the best-known performers because of the periods of unemployment.

Work Environment

Actors work under varying conditions. Those employed in motion pictures may work in air-conditioned studios one week and be on location in a hot desert the next.

Those in stage productions perform under all types of conditions. The number of hours employed per day or week vary, as do the number of weeks employed per year. Stage actors normally perform eight shows per week with any additional performances paid for as overtime. The basic workweek after the show opens is about 36 hours unless major changes in the play are needed. The number of hours worked per week is considerably more before the opening, because of rehearsals. Evening work is a natural part of a stage actor's life. Rehearsals often are held at night and over holidays and weekends. If the play goes on the road, much traveling will be involved.

A number of actors cannot receive unemployment compensation when they are waiting for their next part, primarily because they have not worked enough to meet the minimum eligibility requirements for compensation. Sick leaves and paid vacations are not usually available to the actor. However, union actors who earn the minimum qualifications now receive full medical and health insurance under all the actors' unions. Those who earn health plan benefits for 10 years become eligible for a pension upon retirement. The acting field is very uncertain. Aspirants never know whether they will be able to get into the profession, and, once in, there are uncertainties as to whether the show will be well received and, if not, whether the actors' talent can survive a bad show.

Outlook

Employment in acting is expected to grow faster than the average through 2010, according to the U.S. Department of Labor. There are a number of reasons for this. The growth of satellite and cable television in the past decade has created a demand for more actors, especially as the cable networks produce more and more of their own programs and films. The rise of home video has also created new acting jobs, as more and more films are made strictly for the home video market. Many resorts built in the 1980s and 1990s present their own theatrical productions, providing more job opportunities for actors. Jobs in theater, however, face pressure as the cost of mounting a production rises and as many nonprofit and smaller theaters lose their funding.

Despite the growth in opportunities, there are many more actors than there are roles, and this is likely to remain true for years to come. This is true in all areas of the arts, including radio, television, motion pictures, and theater, and even those who are employed are normally employed during only a small portion of the year. Many actors must supplement their income by working in other areas, such as secretaries, waiters, or taxi drivers, for example. Almost all performers are members of more than one union in order to take advantage of various opportunities as they become available.

It should be recognized that of the 105,000 or so actors in the United States today, an average of only about 16,000 are employed at any one time. Of these, few are able to support themselves on their earnings from acting, and fewer still will ever achieve stardom. Most actors work for many years before becoming known, and most of these do not rise above supporting roles. The vast majority of actors, meanwhile, are still looking for the right break. There are many more applicants in all areas than there are positions. As with most careers in the arts, people enter this career out of a love and desire for acting.

For More Information

The following is a professional union for actors in theater and "live" industrial productions, stage managers, some directors, and choreographers:

Actors' Equity Association
165 West 46th Street, 15th Floor
New York, NY 10036
Tel: 212-869-8530
Web: http://www.actorsequity.org

This union represents television and radio performers, including actors, announcers, dancers, disc jockeys, newspersons, singers, specialty acts, sportscasters, and stuntpersons.

American Federation of Television and Radio Artists
260 Madison Avenue
New York, NY 10016
Tel: 212-532-0800
Web: http://www.aftra.org

A directory of theatrical programs may be purchased from NAST. For answers to a number of frequently asked questions concerning education, visit the NAST Web site.

National Association of Schools of Theater (NAST)
11250 Roger Bacon Drive, Suite 21
Reston, VA 20190
Tel: 703-437-0700
Email: info@arts-accredit.org
Web: http://www.arts-accredit.org/nast

The following union offers information on actors, directors, and producers:

Screen Actors Guild
5757 Wilshire Boulevard
Los Angeles, CA 90036
Tel: 323-954-1600
Web: http://www.sag.com

For information about opportunities in not-for-profit theaters, contact:

Theatre Communications Group
355 Lexington Avenue
New York, NY 10017
Tel: 212-697-5230
Web: http://www.tcg.org

This site has information for beginners on acting and the acting business.

Acting Workshop On-Line
Web: http://www.redbirdstudio.com/AWOL/acting2.html

Circus Performers

School Subjects	Physical education Theater/dance
Personal Skills	Artistic Mechanical/manipulative
Work Environment	Indoors and outdoors Primarily multiple locations
Minimum Education Level	Apprenticeship
Salary Range	$10,000 to $30,000 to $100,000
Certification or Licensing	None available
Outlook	Little change or more slowly than the average

Overview

Circus performers entertain with a wide variety of unusual acts that terrify, amuse, and amaze their audiences. Performers appear to defy death as they swing from a trapeze or walk a tightwire high above the ground. Some perform gymnastic feats on the ground, and clowns entertain with their absurd antics. Others train and perform with animals, such as elephants and tigers. Most circus performers are able to perform a variety of circus skills.

History

The first circus in the United States was established by John Bill Ricketts in Philadelphia in 1793. Ricketts' circus featured equestrian acts, as well as a tightrope walker, a clown, and an acrobatic act. Performances were given inside a ring, which was surrounded by a low fence. Ricketts' troupe toured through most of the northeastern United States until 1800, when Ricketts went to England. By then, the tradition of the circus parade had already been established by a competing circus organized by Philip Lailson. Toward the middle of the 19th century, colorful circus wagons were also included in circus parades. Other traveling circuses toured the United States, although they were not formally called circuses until 1824. These early circuses usually featured equestrian showmanship, and their proprietors were also featured performers.

A new type of circus originated in 1825, when J. Purdy Brown introduced the "big top." Instead of constructing a wooden building in which to perform, Brown erected a large tent or pavilion. The big top could be set up and taken down more easily and moved from location to location every day. In this way, a circus could reach a wider audience. In the 1830s, circuses also added menageries, which featured wild and exotic animals; soon, performers risked their lives by going into the cages of the most ferocious animals.

Circuses grew larger and more varied through the 19th century. More and more circuses were being run by people who did not perform. Noted proprietors in the mid-19th century were Aaron Turner, Rufus Welch, James Raymond, and Gilbert Spalding. Some performers became well-known figures for their acts, such as John Glenroy, who could turn a backwards somersault while riding bareback. Traveling circuses usually spent their winters on the East Coast. This meant that as they traveled they often reached no further than the midwestern territories before being forced to turn back for the winter. In 1847, the Mabie Brothers circus established its winter headquarters in Delavan, Wisconsin. Many other circuses followed this idea, and over the years more than 100 circuses have been founded or have wintered in Wisconsin.

Perhaps the most famous of all circus proprietors entered the scene in 1871. Phineas Taylor Barnum, known as P. T. Barnum, was born in 1810 in Connecticut. For most of his career, Barnum was a showman, featuring acts such as the 161-year-old nurse of George Washington, the "Feejee Mermaid," (which was, in fact, the upper half of a monkey that had been attached to the lower half of a fish), the famous midget Tom Thumb, and others. Barnum, known for the slogan "There's a sucker born every minute," was famous for his elaborate publicity campaigns. From 1848 to 1868, Barnum ran the American Museum in New York City, which specialized in curiosities, wild animals, and "freaks" and was one of the most popular attractions in the country, selling over 40 million tickets.

In 1870, Barnum was approached by circus proprietors William C. Coup and Dan Castello, and the three formed a partnership, renaming the circus the P. T. Barnum Circus. In 1872, Barnum suggested that the circus travel by train, stopping only at the bigger cities, where the audiences were largest. In addition to the big top, Barnum's circus featured a sideshow and museum and was advertised heavily before every performance. By the end of the 1870s, there were 25 traveling circuses, the largest traveling by train; by

1905, more than 100 circuses toured the United States. The circus had become the most popular form of entertainment.

A large circus could fill 60 railroad cars and had big top tents more than 500 feet long, capable of seating as many as 10,000 people. Until 1872, circuses still featured a single performance area, or ring; two-ring circuses appeared in the 1870s, and the three-ring circus appeared in 1882. Performances grew more and more spectacular, with the flying trapeze, aerial gymnastics, human cannonball acts, and other death-defying feats. In 1891, wild animal acts moved under the big top, presented by Miss Carlotta and Colonel Boone of the Adam Forepaugh Circus.

James A. Bailey was another renowned circus owner. In 1880, the first live birth of an elephant in captivity occurred at Bailey's Great London Circus, and the baby elephant became a huge attraction. Bailey and P. T. Barnum soon became partners. They brought over an African elephant named "Jumbo," which was billed as the largest animal on Earth and became the biggest circus attraction of the day. Another elephant, the so-called "white elephant," was so widely publicized that the term has entered our vocabulary.

The five Ringling Brothers from Baraboo, Wisconsin, organized their first circus in 1884. By 1890, their circus had grown large enough to become a railroad show, and by the end of the century, the Ringling Brothers' Circus was one of the largest in the United States. In 1888, P. T. Barnum took the Barnum & Bailey Circus and its *Greatest Show on Earth* to England, where people went as much to see P. T. Barnum himself as they did to see the circus.

After Barnum's death in 1891, and Bailey's death in 1903, the Ringling Brothers bought the Barnum & Bailey Circus in 1907. For the next 10 years, the two circuses operated separately. But in 1919, the shows were merged into the most well-known circus of all, Ringling Brothers and Barnum & Bailey Circus, which featured a wide array of performances, from bareback riding to the flying trapeze to feats of strength, and included the famous Flying Walendas.

While the largest circuses traveled by railroad, there were many smaller circuses still performing in the smaller cities and towns. The development of the automobile and a paved road system soon allowed these circuses to travel more quickly and to more places than ever before, and by the 1920s, the first successful truck circuses were traveling the country. By the 1950s, most circuses, especially the tented circuses such as the Clyde Beatty Circus, traveled by truck. Others, including the Ringling Brothers and Barnum & Bailey Circus, no longer used a tent at all, but performed instead inside the largest arenas and auditoriums.

Modern circuses are more varied than ever before. Circus performers often become famous celebrities, such as Dolly Jacobs, who amazed audiences by performing somersaults on the Roman Rings; Miquel Vasquez, the originator of the quadruple somersault on the flying trapeze; and Gunther Gebel-Williams, whose world-famous animal act included tigers, leopards, elephants, and horses.

Today there are some 40 traveling circuses in the United States and many more throughout the world. In the 1980s, Cirque du Soleil of Canada created a new type of circus, featuring elaborately choreographed dance, music, lighting, and costumes to augment its stage performances.

The Job

Circus historian George Chindahl has identified as many as 200 different circus acts, and new ones are being created every day. Some circus performers work alone, although most work as part of a troupe. Every performer, whether solo or a group, develops a unique act. The aim is to amaze, entertain, and thrill the audience with their performances, which often feature risky, even death-defying, stunts. A great deal of a performance is the suspense created until the performer is once again safe on the ground. When not performing, the performers and their apprentices and other helpers maintain their equipment, oversee the set-up of the equipment, maintain their costumes and other props used during performances, and train and rehearse their routines.

At the beginning of the circus show, all the performers join in the circus parade around the arena. Performers wait backstage during the show until it is time for them to perform. They usually wait near the entrances, so that they are ready to go on as soon as they are called. Circus shows may feature 20 or more separate acts, and each performance and the entire show are precisely timed.

Aerialists perform vaulting, leaping, and flying acts, such as trapeze, rings, and cloud swings. Balancing acts include wire walkers and acrobats. *Jugglers* handle a variety of objects, such as clubs, balls, or hoops and perform on the ground or on a high wire. *Aquatic performers* perform water stunts, usually only in very large circuses. *Animal trainers* work with lions, tigers, bears, elephants, or horses. These performers almost always own and care for the animals they work with. *Clowns* dress in outlandish costumes, paint their faces, and use a variety of performance skills to entertain audiences. *Circus musicians and conductors* play in bands, called windjammers, which provide dramatic and comedic accompaniment for all acts. Each act has its own music, and the windjammers cue each act as it begins its music. Other common circus entertainers are daredevil performers and trick bicyclists.

Almost all circus performers combine several skills, and may participate in more than one act during a show. All circus acts are physically demanding, requiring strength, endurance, and flexibility.

Circus work is seasonal. Performers work during the spring, summer, and fall, giving perhaps two or three shows a day on weekends and holidays. Some circuses, such as Ringling Brothers, perform from February to November. During the winter months, they train, improve their acts, or work in sponsored indoor circuses. Circus performers sometimes take jobs on stage while not in season. Many circus performers develop variety acts that they can perform in places like Las Vegas or on cruise ships.

Circus performers can spend up to 10 years in training. Once they have developed their act, they may join a circus for one or several seasons, or they may travel from circus to circus as independent acts. In either case, there is a great deal of travel involved.

Requirements

High School

There are no educational requirements for circus performers. Those who have a high school or college education, however, will have an advantage because they will be better able to manage their business affairs and communicate with others. Knowledge of foreign languages will be helpful for performers hoping to travel overseas.

Athletic training that develops coordination, strength, and balance is necessary for almost all circus performers and should be developed at a young age. Other training includes acting, music, dance, and for those interested in animals, veterinary care. Animal trainers usually must complete a long apprenticeship.

Postsecondary Training

Most circus performers learn their skills as apprentices to well-established acts. There are a few skills that can be learned on your own in a few weeks or months, such as juggling, unicycling, and puppetry, but most circus skills take many years to learn and perfect. Most circus performers develop skills in two or more areas, which makes them more attractive to employers.

Depending on your interests, you can receive some formal training in a number of areas. The San Francisco School of Circus Arts (http://www.sfcircus.org), for example, is open to the public and offers classes in juggling, flying trapeze, and contortion, among other activities. The Dell'Arte International School of Physical Theatre (http://www.dellarte.com), in Blue Lake, California, while not a circus arts school, does offer classes in physical theater useful for anyone interested in clowning, miming, and relating to audiences through performance. If you would like to combine a college education with circus experience, consider attending Florida State University, home of the FSU Flying High Circus (http://www.fsu.edu/~circus). This circus is an extracurricular activity open to Florida State students in good standing and provides the opportunity to work in any area of the circus that interests you. The majority of circus performers begin their careers as children, as members of performing families.

Other Requirements

Circus performers must be physically fit and must be able to withstand the rigors of their act as well as the hardships of constant travel. Some acts require unusual strength, flexibility, or balance.

Exploring

If circus performance interests you, see a circus. Go to every circus that comes to your area. Talk to the performers about their work. Ask outright if there are jobs available, or write to circuses to express your interest in finding circus work.

Gymnastics teams, drama clubs, and dance troupes provide performance experience and may help you decide if you have talent for this type of work. Those interested in animal training should volunteer at nearby zoos or stables. Ballet and mime are also valuable sources of insight into this field.

You may wish to join an association of jugglers, unicyclists, or another specialty. They often hold festivals, events, and seminars where you can train, get to know other circus performers, and perhaps find a mentor who can help you get into the field.

Attending a circus camp is also an excellent way to learn skills and find out about this career. Camps, such as Circus Camp in Georgia (http://www.circuscamp.org) and Circus Smirkus (http://www.circussmirkus.org) in Vermont, are available across the country, and you can find out about them by searching the Web with the words "circus camp." In addition to being a camper, you may be able to find summer work as a counselor or instructor at such a camp once you have some experience.

Employers

While it goes without saying that circus performers are largely employed by traveling circuses, they are being used in a variety of other venues, including stage shows, nightclubs, casinos, on Broadway, and on television. As with many other performing arts professions, more opportunities of this type are available in larger cities, especially those that appeal to tourists, such as New York, Los Angeles, and Las Vegas.

Starting Out

Circus performers usually enter the field through one of four methods. First, they may join a circus in a relatively low position and work their way up through the ranks. One option for someone joining the circus this way is to look at the Web sites of larger circuses, such as Big Apple Circus, for job openings. Those who enter the circus profession this way, known as "walkons," may start as part of a set-up or clean-up crew, or they may care for animals. Then, as they get to know performers, they become apprentices. After learning the necessary skills, they gradually work their way into the act.

The second way is to purchase an existing act. Beginners do not usually start with this method. The buyer often receives training, costumes, and equipment as a condition of purchase.

The third method is to enter a preprofessional program that offers a placement service once training is completed. There are very few of these programs in the United States.

The fourth method is to be raised in a circus performing family. Most circus performers enter the field by this method. From 75 to 90 percent of all circus performers come from circus performing families.

Most circus performers develop their acts and then hire an agent who finds work for them. There are only a few agents in the United States who specialize in circus acts. Performers have to audition for potential employers the agent finds.

Circus performers counsel that it is wise to get as much work in as many different places as you can and to not limit your skills. Develop a specialty or gimmick, but learn several skills. Most circus owners look for performers who can perform a variety of acts during a single show.

Advancement

It helps if an aspiring circus performer is born into a circus family and they can begin training as soon as they are able to walk. Later, they will be incorporated into the family's act and as they get older, they will take a more and more prominent position. But many successful circus performers started at the bottom as laborers and learned their skills by watching. Once performers have developed skill in a variety of areas, they gain journeyman status and may set out on their own, acquire their act from the performer who trained them, join an established act, or form a new act with others. Those with the most unusual and unique acts and skills may find themselves in great demand and can sign long-term contracts with a circus.

Some circus performers become quite famous and can command large sums of money. Some circus performers enter other performing areas, such as the stage, Broadway, Las Vegas variety shows, and television programs and commercials.

Earnings

Earnings for circus performers vary so widely that it is difficult to determine the average salaries. It is clear, however, that people entering this field do so out of love and not for the money.

According to the Circus World Museum, those just starting out usually do not earn much more than the minimum wage, and sometimes even lower, perhaps $200 to $400 per week. Generally, however, they are provided with food and lodging while they complete their training, which may last 10 years or more. Those on the lower level of performing, such as showgirls and clowns, may jump to $600 to $700 per week, while those whose acts involve animals may earn from several thousand per week up to $100,000 or more for the circus season. The amount performers earn depends on a number of factors, but especially the degree of fame or recognition they achieve. Performers who develop highly unusual and distinctive acts stand the best chance of higher earnings. Star performers may sign multi-year contracts for many millions of dollars.

Salaries also range widely among the different circuses. Some circuses, like Cirque du Soleil, pay their performers quite well. Performers at Ringling Brothers, on the other hand, may accept lower pay because the Ringling Brothers' fame more than compensates for the lower salaries, and gaining experience at Ringling Brothers means that they can later command higher salaries elsewhere.

Circus performers often pay for their own transportation and manage their own business affairs. Rarely do they get a paid vacation.

Work Environment

Circus performers work long hours performing, and even longer hours preparing their acts. The learning and relearning periods are intense and physically demanding. Heavy travel is involved and most acts require expensive equipment, props, and costumes.

Circus performers enjoy being able to choose their engagements and be their own bosses. They have the freedom to create their own art form that showcases their particular talent. They face the continual challenge of creating new routines never done before.

Outlook

P. T. Barnum once said, "As long as there are children, there will always be circuses." Circuses will continue, though their formats change with the times.

Traditional circuses are changing. Tents are seldom used because they are costly and impractical. It's often more convenient to perform in an arena. Also, many animal acts are being eliminated because of the large costs involved in maintaining and transporting them. There is less emphasis on props and equipment, to make travel easier and cheaper. Circus acts are more flexible: they are able to perform in either a three-ring format or on a proscenium stage. Circuses are becoming more theatrical, using professional designers, lighting, and musicians. They often have a special theme. Specialty circuses are expanding, such as Cirque du Soleil, Big Apple Circus, and Circus Flora.

Those who work in a resident company of a circus can become well known and have greater job security. There are more opportunities for circus performers outside the circus, and there is always an interest for new, unusual, never-been-seen acts. The private party business is growing, and circus performers may be used in television and music videos. Even with the changes, the popularity of circuses has remained steady and should remain so for the next 10 years.

The number of circus performers far outnumbers the job openings. More and more circus acts from overseas, especially from Eastern Europe, Russia, and China, are competing for openings in American circuses. In addition, the rise of animal activism has made the development of acts involving animals more challenging. So while opportunities remain good for highly skilled performers, they are marginal for those at the entry level.

For More Information

This circus travels across the country providing education programs to schools, businesses, and other groups. Visit its Web site to find out where the troupe is now and the programs offered.

Circus of the Kids
926 Waverly Road
Tallahassee, FL 32312
Tel: 866-247-2875
Web: http://www.circusofthekids.com

To learn more about circuses of the past as well as the present, visit Circus World Museum. If you can't make it in person, check out its Web site.

Circus World Museum
550 Water Street
Baraboo, WI 53913
Tel: 608-356-8341
Web: http://www.circusworldmuseum.com

This Web site offers facts and information about Ringling Brothers and Barnum & Bailey circus, including news, games, animals, history and tradition, performers, and show dates.

Ringling Brothers and Barnum & Bailey
8607 Westwood Center Drive
Vienna, VA 22182
Tel: 608-278-0520
Web: http://www.ringling.com

Circus Fans Association of America works to preserve circuses. Members receive The White Tops *magazine with information on current circus acts, performers, marketing ideas, and other industry news. The Web site includes information on treatment of circus animals, membership, and links to circus-related sites.*

Circus Fans Association of America
Web: http://www.circusfans.org

Comedians

English Theater/dance	School Subjects
Artistic Communication/ideas	Personal Skills
Primarily indoors Primarily multiple locations	Work Environment
High school diploma	Minimum Education Level
$6,000 to $30,000 to $200,000+	Salary Range
None available	Certification or Licensing
About as fast as the average	Outlook

Overview

Comedians are entertainers who make people laugh. They use a variety of techniques to amuse their audiences, including telling jokes, composing and singing humorous songs, wearing funny costumes, and doing impersonations. Comedians perform in nightclubs, comedy clubs, coffeehouses, theaters, television shows, films, and even business functions, such as trade shows and sales meetings.

History

Throughout history, people have enjoyed humorous interpretations of the events that make up their daily lives. Comedy began as a type of drama that presented events in a comic way and thereby sought to amuse its audience. These dramas were not always funny, yet they were usually lighthearted and had happy endings (as opposed to tragedies, which had sad endings).

The Greeks and Romans had playwrights such as Aristophanes (450?-380? BC) and Plautus (254?-184? BC) who successfully used humor as a type of mirror on the social and political customs of the time. They wrote plays that highlighted some of the particularities of the rich and powerful as well as common people. An early type of comedian was the *fool* or *jester* attached to a royal court, whose function was to entertain by singing, dancing, telling jokes, riddles, and humorous stories, and even by impersonating the king and other members of the aristocracy. In later years, English playwright William Shakespeare (1564-1616) and French playwright Moliere (1622-73) used wit and humor to point out some of the shortcomings of society.

In the 19th century, as cities became more and more crowded, comedy became an especially important diversion for people. During this time, minstrel, burlesque, and vaudeville shows became very popular. These shows usually featured a combination of song, comedy, and other acts, such as magic or acrobatics. Many of the popular comedians of the 20th century began their careers in burlesque and vaudeville, and hundreds of theaters opened in the United States catering to this form of entertainment. A distinctive part of vaudeville was the great variety of acts presented during a single show. Comedians especially had to work hard to catch the audience's attention and make themselves memorable among the other performers. Vaudeville provided a training ground for many of the most popular comedians of the 20th century, including stars such as Bud Abbott and Lou Costello, Milton Berle, Mae West, Bob Hope, the Marx Brothers, George Burns and Gracie Allen, W. C. Fields, and Will Rogers.

Vaudeville soon faced competition from the film industry. People flocked to motion pictures as a new form of entertainment, and many of the vaudeville theaters closed or converted to showing films. For comedians, the new form of entertainment proved ideal for their craft. During the early years of cinema, slapstick films starring the Keystone Cops, Buster Keaton, Charlie Chaplin, Fatty Arbuckle, and many others became immensely popular. Radio also provided a venue for many comedians, and people would gather around a living room radio to hear the performances of stars such as Milton Berle, Edgar Bergen, Jack Benny, and Jimmy Durante. When sound was added to the films in the late 1920s and early 1930s, comedians were able to adapt their stand-up and radio routines to film and many numbered among the most popular stars in the United States and throughout the world.

Later, television provided another venue for comedians. Milton Berle was one of the very first television stars. *The Ed Sullivan Show* became an important place for comedians to launch their acts to a national audience. Many comedians developed their own television shows, and many more comedians found work writing jokes and scripts for this comedic medium.

Stand-up comedy, that is, live performances before an audience, continues to be one of the most important ways for a comedian to develop an act and perfect timing, delivery, and other skills. Stand-up comedians do more than simply make people laugh; they attempt to make people think. Current events continue to provide a rich source for material, and the stand-up comedian has become a social critic who uses humor as the medium for the message. For example, in the early 1960s, Lenny Bruce caused a great deal of controversy in the United States by using his nightclub routines to question the role of organized religion in society and to argue against censorship. During the 1960s, comedians, such as members of The Second City theater group based in Chicago, began to adapt improvisational acting techniques, creating a new form of comedic theater. Many of these comedy actors, including John Belushi and Shelley Long, went on to stardom.

Stand-up comedy continues to provide an important training ground for comedians. Most of the biggest comedy stars, such as Steve Martin, Jerry Seinfeld, Roseanne, Richard Pryor, Tim Allen, Eddie Murphy, Ellen Degeneres, and many others had their starts as stand-up comedians. During the 1980s, hundreds of new comedy clubs opened across the country, providing more venues for comedians to hone their craft than ever before.

The Job

Although making people laugh may sound like a pretty simple assignment, comedians work very hard at this task. Because there are many types of comedy, from physical and slapstick to comedy involving highly sophisticated wordplay, all comedians must develop their own style. Comedians may appear in regular attire or incorporate colorful costumes, music, props, or other techniques into their act. In any case, it is generally the writing and timing that makes a comedian unique.

Perhaps the most common form of comedic performer is the stand-up comic. *Stand-up comedians* usually perform in nightclubs or comedy clubs, entertaining audiences with jokes, stories, and impersonations. Most often, stand-up comics write their own material, so they spend a great deal of time developing, perfecting, and rehearsing new material. Adding new bits and creating entirely new routines provides a constant challenge for the comedian.

Stand-up comedians often travel around the country, performing in a variety of settings. They may have to adapt their performances somewhat, depending on the audience. The length of the performance is determined by whether the comedian is the main act or an opening act. A main act will last from 30 minutes to an hour, while an opening act may be just a few minutes.

Another popular type of performance is improvisation, often abbreviated to "improv." *Improv comedians* work without a set routine and make up their own dialogue as they go along. It allows for a kind of spontaneity that traditional performances do not. Improv groups perform skits, dances, and songs using well-trained comedic creativity. Many comedy groups will perform a number of scripted skits and then improvise a number of skits based on audience suggestions.

Comedians are storytellers. No matter where they perform, their goal is to engage their audience through various characters and stories. Many comedians use their own life stories as material, weaving a picture of people and places designed not only to evoke laughter but also understanding.

Comedians may perform their work live or on tape. Usually a taping is done in front of an audience, as comedians need the laughter and other feedback of an audience to be most effective.

Comedians who perform on film or television have the same restrictions as other actors and actresses. They must adhere to strict schedules and perform routines repeatedly before the director decides a scene is finished. Film and television comedians usually perform scenes that someone else has written. They are required to memorize their lines and rehearse their performances.

As with other performance artists, comedians often find themselves looking for employment. Comedians may work for a number of weeks in a row and then face a period of unemployment. To find work, many comedians hire booking agents to locate club owners willing to hire them. Many clubs feature open mike nights, in which anyone may perform, providing important opportunities for beginning comedians. Other comedians attempt to find work on their own. A person's success in finding work will be largely influenced by skill and style, but also to an extent by personal contacts and a bit of good fortune.

For comedians who are uncomfortable in front of an audience, there is the opportunity to write material for other performers. Not all people who write comedic material are former comedians, but all understand the fundamental elements of humor and ways of using words and images to make people laugh.

Requirements

High School

There are no set educational standards for comedians. The overriding requirement is to be funny. Comedians should also have a love of performing and a strong desire to make people laugh.

A comedian should obviously have good communications skills and be able to write their material in a succinct and humorous manner. It is also necessary to have a strong stage presence. Often, budding comedians will take English and composition classes, as well as speech and acting courses, to help develop skills in these areas. Accounting and bookkeeping skills are also helpful, as comedians often prepare their own financial records.

Postsecondary Training

Few colleges and universities offer specific courses on how to become a comedian. However, higher education may give a comedian a stronger understanding of society and current events, useful when writing their material. Becoming a comedian takes a lot of hard work and, as with other performance skills, practice, practice, practice. Many communities have improvisational groups that provide a training ground for aspiring actors and comedians. Some comedy clubs also offer classes.

Other Requirements

Making people laugh is not a skill that is easily taught. Most good comedians have an inborn talent and have made jokes or performed humorous skits since childhood. This means more than simply being the class clown; talented comedians see events in a humorous light and share this perspective with others. Above all else, a comedian must have a keen sense of timing. A funny line, delivered improperly, loses its effectiveness.

Comedians come in all shapes and sizes. Indeed, it is often the person who looks and feels somewhat different who is better able to see humorous aspects of human nature and society. A comedian should be able to take material from his or her own background (be it growing up in a small town, having overbearing parents, or other situations) and interpret this material in a way that appeals to others.

Comedians should be keen observers of daily life and be perceptive enough to recognize the humor in everyday events. But comedians cannot be disappointed if audiences do not respond to their jokes at every performance. It may take years to develop the skills to be a successful comedian, and even the most successful comedians can have an off night.

Exploring

The field of comedy offers a number of good opportunities for career exploration. For example, many improvisational groups offer classes in acting and performance techniques. These groups are often highly competitive, but they are a good place to learn skills, make contacts, and have fun. Of course, there is no substitute for hands-on experience, and most comedy clubs and coffee houses have open mike nights where aspiring comedians can get on stage and try out their material in front of a real audience. To get an idea of what it is like to perform before an audience, aspiring comedians can also stage performances for family and friends before venturing on stage to perform for strangers. Acting in school plays and local productions is another good way to get performing experience. It is also possible to learn by watching others. Visit a comedy club or coffee house to observe comedians at work. Try to talk informally with a comedian to learn more about the profession. Finally, do some research. There are also a number of books that describe exercises and techniques for comedians.

Employers

Comedians work in a wide variety of venues, including comedy clubs, resorts, hotels, and cruise ships. Television networks, especially cable television, are major employers of comedians. They hire comedians not just as performers, but as writers for situation comedies, movies, and talk shows, and as entertainers for the audiences at live tapings. A comedian interested in performing is well advised to hire an agent to find employers and book engagements.

Starting Out

Getting started as a comedian is often very difficult. There are thousands of people who want to make people laugh, but relatively few venues for aspiring comedians to get exposure. To find an opportunity to perform, you may have to repeatedly call local nightclubs, bars, or coffee houses. Generally, these clubs will already have a number of comedians they use.

A common way to get a first break is to attend open mike nights and call for auditions at a local club. These auditions are not private showings for club owners, but rather actual performances in front of audiences. Usually, comedians are not paid at these auditions, but those who show the most promise are often invited back to put on paid performances.

Another way to break into the career is through a comedy improvisational group. These groups offer novice comedians a chance to refine skills, developing techniques and contacts before starting out on their own. However, joining many of these groups can be highly competitive; often, an aspiring comedian may join a lesser-known improv group while working on skills and auditioning for better-known groups.

Another way to get a start in comedy is through acting. Actors with a flair for comedy can audition for film comedies and situation comedy series. Much of the cast of the hit comedy series *Friends,* for example, came from an acting background.

Advancement

Comedians who find success at local clubs or as part of an improvisation group can go on to perform at larger clubs and theaters. Some may also find work in the corporate world, entertaining at trade shows and other meetings. Extremely successful comedians may go on to tape comedy routines for broadcast or even have their own television shows.

Comedians can also branch out somewhat in their career goals. Some choose to write material for other comedians or review comedic performances for the local media. Others become comedy club owners or talent agents, creating employment opportunities for other comedians.

Comedy writers may go on to work for advertising agencies, using humor as a means of creating commercials or other promotional materials. Others may develop television or movie scripts.

Earnings

People who only look at the incomes of well-known comedians will get a mistaken notion of how much comedians earn. Jim Carrey may earn millions for a single movie, other comedy stars may earn $200,000 for one performance, but the vast majority of comedians earn far lower wages. In fact, most comedians must hold full- or part-time jobs to supplement the income from their performances.

In large comedy clubs, a headline comedian can expect to earn between $1,000 and $20,000 per show, depending on his or her drawing power. Those who perform as an opening act might earn between $125 and $350 per show. Headline comedians at smaller clubs will earn between $300 and $800 per show. Comedians hired to perform college shows earn around $500 per show. Of course, those just starting out will earn very little (remember, most club owners do not pay comedians who are auditioning), and start at as little as $15 to $20 dollars for a 20-minute set. Despite this meager pay, beginners working in clubs will be in a good position to learn the craft and make valuable contacts.

Comedians who entertain at trade shows and sales meetings can earn several hundred dollars per show, yet these assignments tend to be infrequent.

Comedy writers have a very wide pay scale. Those who write for well-known comedians are paid about $50 for every joke used. (Of course, many jokes are rejected by the performer.) Full-time comedy writers for the *Tonight Show* and other television shows can expect to earn between $50,000 and $150,000 per year, depending on their skill, experience, and the budget of the show.

Work Environment

Full-time comedians usually spend a lot of time traveling between shows. A comedian may have a strong following in the Midwest, for example, and in the course of a week have two shows in Detroit, two shows in Chicago, and a show in St. Louis. Some people may find this lifestyle exciting, but for many it is exhausting and lonely. Those who perform as part of an improv troupe may also travel a lot. Once a comedian has developed a good following, the traveling may subside somewhat. More established comedians perform at one or two clubs in the same city on a fairly regular basis.

Performing in front of an audience can be very demanding. Not all audiences are receptive (especially to new material) and a comedian may encounter unresponsive crowds. It is also not uncommon for comedians to perform for small audiences in bars and nightclubs. Many of these nightclubs may be small, dark, and filled with smoke.

Despite these challenges, comedians can have fascinating careers. They experience the thrill of performing in front of audiences, and positively affecting people's lives. Comedians may go on to achieve a good deal of fame, especially those who perform on television or in the movies. As creative artists, comedians may find it very satisfying to express their views and get positive feedback from others. There can be a lot of pleasure in making people laugh and seeing others enjoy themselves.

Comedians usually work late into the night, often not starting performances until 9 or 10 PM. They also generally work weekends, when people have more time to go to nightclubs and comedy clubs.

Part-time comedians often hold day jobs and perform at night. Similarly, comedy writers may have to work other jobs to make ends meet financially. They might prepare material in their homes or in small offices with other writers.

Outlook

As with the other performance arts, there will always be more aspiring comedians then there are job opportunities. However, comedians enjoy more solid employment prospects than actors or actresses. There are hundreds of comedy clubs across the country (usually in larger cities) and each club needs performers to get their audiences laughing. During the 1990s, the boom in comedy clubs slowed. However, more recently, new venues such as casinos, resorts, and theme parks, continue to offer new opportunities for comedians. Of course, the most lucrative jobs will go to those with the best reputation, but thousands of comedians will continue to find steady work in the next decade.

There is also a growing trend for private companies to hire comedians to perform at sales meetings and trade shows. Comedians help to increase interest in products and create an enjoyable sales environment. Talent agencies now increasingly book comedians to work at these events.

For those who choose to work as comedy writers or entertainment critics, the competition for jobs should be keen, yet there are good career opportunities. The growth of the cable television industry in particular has created a need for increasing numbers of writers to work on the growing number of new shows. There are a large number of comedy shows on the national networks and on cable television, and these should provide a good market for skilled comedy writers.

For More Information

For information on theaters, training centers, and famous alumni, contact:

The Second City
1616 North Wells Street
Chicago, IL 60614
Tel: 312-664-4032
Web: http://www.secondcity.com

Composers

Music Theater/dance	School Subjects
Artistic Communication/ideas	Personal Skills
Primarily indoors Primarily one location	Work Environment
High school diploma	Minimum Education Level
$2,000 to $31,510 to $1,000,000+	Salary Range
None available	Certification or Licensing
About as fast as the average	Outlook

Overview

Composers create much of the music heard every day on radio and television, in theaters and concert halls, on recordings and in advertising, and through any other medium of musical presentation. Composers write symphonies, concertos, and operas; scores for theater, television, and cinema; and music for musical theater, recording artists, and commercial advertising. They may combine elements of classical music with elements of popular musical styles such as rock, jazz, reggae, folk, and others.

History

Classical (used in the widest sense) composition probably dates back to the late Middle Ages, when musical notation began to develop in Christian monasteries. In those times and for some centuries thereafter, the church was the main patron of musical composition. During the 14th century, or possibly earlier, the writing of music in score (that is, for several instruments or instruments and voices) began to take place. This was the beginning of orchestral writing. Composers then were mostly sponsored by the church and were supposed to be religiously motivated in their work, which was not to be considered an expression of their own emotions. It was probably not until the end of the 15th century that the work of a composer began to be recognized as a statement of individual expression. Recognition of composers did not really become common until several centuries later. Even Johann Sebastian Bach (1685-1750), writing in the 18th century, was known more as an organist and choirmaster during his lifetime.

The writing of music in score was the beginning of a great change in the history of music. The craft of making musical instruments and the techniques of playing them were advancing also. By the beginning of the Baroque Period, around 1600, these changes brought musical composition to a new stage of development, which was enhanced by patronage from secular sources. The nobility had taken an interest in sponsoring musical composition, and over the next two to three hundred years they came to supplant the church as the main patrons of composers. Under their patronage, composers had more room to experiment and develop new musical styles.

During the Baroque Period, which lasted until about 1750, there was a flowering of musical forms, including opera. In the early 1600s, Rome became preeminent in opera, using the chorus and dance to embellish the operatic spectacle. Instrumental music also grew during the Baroque Period, reaching its greatest flowering in the work of Johann Sebastian Bach and George Frederick Handel (1685-1759). The major musical forms of Baroque origin were the sonata and cantata, both largely attributed to the composers of opera.

The "true" Classical Period in music began in about the mid-18th century and lasted through the 19th century. Composers embellishing the sonata form now developed the symphony. Through the latter half of the 19th century, most composers of symphonies, concerti, chamber music, and other instrumental forms adhered to the strict formality of the Classical tradition. In the 19th century, however, many composers broke from Classical formalism, instilling greater emotionalism, subjectivity, and individualism in their work. The new musical style evolved into what became formally known as the Romantic movement in music. Romanticism did not replace classicism, but rather, existed side by side with the older form. A transitional figure in the break from classicism was Ludwig van Beethoven (1770-1827), whose compositions elevated the symphonic form to its highest level. Other composers who perfected the Romantic style included Franz Schubert (1797-1828), Franz Liszt (1811-86), Johannes Brahms (1833-97), Hector Berlioz (1803-69), and Peter Ilich Tchaikovsky (1840-93) in orchestral music, and Giuseppe Verdi (1813-1901) and Richard Wagner (1813-83) in opera.

Many of the composers of the early Classical Period labored for little more than recognition. Their monetary rewards were often meager. In the 19th century, however, as the stature of the composers grew, they were able to gain more control over their own work and the proceeds that it produced. The opera composers, in particular, were able to reap quite handsome profits.

Another abrupt break from tradition occurred at the beginning of the 20th century. At that time composers began to turn away from Romanticism and seek new and original styles and sounds. Audiences sometimes were repulsed by these new musical sounds, but eventually they were accepted and imitated by other composers. One of the most successful of the post-Romantic composers was Igor Stravinsky (1882-1971), whose landmark work *The Rite of Spring* was hailed by some to be the greatest work of the century.

Through the 20th century composers continued to write music in the styles of the past and to experiment with new styles. Some contemporary composers, such as George Gershwin (1898-1937) and Leonard Bernstein (1918-90), wrote for both the popular and serious audiences. John Cage (1912-95), Philip Glass (1937-), Steve Reich (1936-), and other composers moved even further from traditional forms and musical instruments, experimenting with electronically created music, in which an electronic instrument, such as a synthesizer, is used to compose and play music. An even more significant advance is the use of computers as a compositional tool. In the 21st century, the only thing predictable in musical composition is that experimentation and change are certain to continue.

The Job

Composers express themselves in music much as writers express themselves with words and painters with line, shape, and color. Composing is hard work. Although influenced by what they hear, composers' compositions are original because they reflect their own interpretation and use of musical elements. All composers use the same basic musical elements, including harmony, melody, counterpoint, and rhythm, but each composer applies these elements in a unique way. Music schools teach all of the elements that go into composition, providing composers with the tools needed for their work, but how a composer uses these tools to create music is what sets an individual apart.

There is no prescribed way for a composer to go about composing. All composers work in a somewhat different way, but generally speaking they pursue their work in some kind of regular, patterned way, in much the same fashion of a novelist or a painter. Composers may work in different areas of classical music, writing, for example, symphonies, operas, concerti, music for a specific instrument or grouping of instruments, and for voice. Many composers also work in popular music, and incorporate popular music ideas in their classical compositions.

Composers may create compositions out of sheer inspiration, with or without a particular market in mind, or they may be commissioned to write a piece of music for a particular purpose. Composers who write music on their own then have the problem of finding someone to perform their music in the hopes that it will be well received and lead to further performances and possibly a recording. The more a composer's music is played and record-ed, the greater the chances to sell future offerings and to receive commissions for new work. Commissions come from institutions (where the composer may or may not be a faculty member), from societies and associations, and orchestral groups, or from film, television, and commercial projects. Almost every film has a score, the music playing throughout the film apart from any songs that may also be in the film.

A composer who wishes to make a living by writing music should understand the musical marketplace as well as possible. It should be under-stood that only a small percentage of music composers can make their living solely by writing music. To make a dent in the marketplace one should be familiar with its major components:

Performance. Composers usually rely on one of two ways to have their music performed: they contact musical performers or producers who are most likely to be receptive to their style of composition, or they may write for a musical group in which they are performers.

Music publishing. Music publishers seek composers who are talented and whose work they feel it will be profitable to promote. They take a cut of the royalties, but they relieve composers of all of the business and legal detail of their profession. Composers today have rather commonly turned to self-publishing.

Copying. A musical composition written for several pieces or voices requires copying into various parts. Composers may do this work them-selves, but it is an exacting task for which professional copiers may be employed. Many composers themselves take on copying work as a sideline.

Computerization. Computers have become an increasingly important tool for composing and copying. Some composers have set up incredibly sophisticated computerized studios in which they compose, score, and play an orchestrated piece by computer. They can also do the copying and pro-duce a recording. Perhaps the most significant enhancement to the home stu-dio is the Musical Instrument Digital Interface (MIDI), which transposes the composer's work into computer language and then converts it into notation.

Recording. Knowing the recording industry is an important aspect in advancing a composer's career. An unrecognized composer will find it difficult to catch on with a commercial recording company, but it is not uncommon for a composer to make his own recording and handle the distribution and promotion as well.

Film and television. There is a very large market for original compositions in feature and industrial films, television programs, and videos. The industry is in constant need of original scores and thematic music.

Students interested in composing can tap into any number of organizations and associations for more detail on any area of musical composition. One such organization providing support and information is Meet the Composer, which is headquartered in New York City and has several national affiliates.

Requirements

High School

There is no specific course of training that leads one to become a composer. Many composers begin composing from a very early age, and receive tutoring and training to encourage their talent. Musically inclined students should continue their private studies and take advantage of everything musical their high school offers. Specially gifted students usually find their way to schools or academies that specialize in music or the arts. These students may begin learning composition in this special environment, and some might begin to create original compositions.

Postsecondary Training

After high school, musical students can continue their education in any of numerous colleges and universities or special music schools or conservatories that offer bachelor's and higher degrees. The composer's course of study includes courses on music history, music criticism, music theory, harmony, counterpoint, rhythm, melody, and ear training. In most major music schools courses in composition are offered along with orchestration and arranging. Courses are also taught covering voice and the major musical instruments, including keyboard, guitar, and, more recently, synthesizer. Most schools now cover computer techniques as applied to music, as well. It may also be helpful to learn at least one foreign language; German, French, and Italian are good choices.

Other Requirements

Prospective composers are advised to become proficient on at least one instrument.

None of this is to say that study in a musical institution is required for a composer, or is any guarantee of success. Some say that composing cannot be taught, that the combination of skills, talent, and inspiration required to create music is a highly individual occurrence. Authorities have argued on both sides of this issue without resolution. It does appear that genetics plays a strong part in musical ability; musical people often come from musical families. There are many contradictions of this, however, and some authorities site the musical environment as being highly influential. The great composers were extraordinarily gifted, and it is very possible that even achieving moderate success in music requires special talent. Nevertheless, there will be little success without hard work and dedication.

Exploring

Musical programs offered by local schools, YMCAs, and community centers offer good beginning opportunities. It is especially helpful to learn to play a musical instrument, such as the piano, violin, or cello. Attending concerts and recitals and reading about music and musicians and their careers will also provide good background and experience. There are also any number of videos available through schools and libraries that teach young people about music. Young musicians should form or join musical groups and attempt to write music for the groups to perform. There are also many books that provide good reference information on careers in composing.

Employers

Composers are self-employed. They complete their work in their own studios and then try to sell their pieces to music publishers, film and television production companies, or recording companies. Once their work becomes well known, clients, such as film and television producers, dance companies, or musical theater producers, may commission original pieces from composers. In this case, the client provides a story line, time period, mood, and other specifications the composer must honor in the creation of a musical score.

There might be a few "house" composer jobs in advertising agencies or studios that make commercials, or at film, television, and video production studios. Schools often underwrite a composer in residence, and many composers work as professors in college and university music departments while continuing to compose. For the most part, however, composers are on their own to create and promote their work.

Starting Out

In school, young composers should try to have their work performed either at school concerts or by local school or community ensembles. This will also most likely involve the composers in copying and scoring their work and possibly even directing. Student film projects can provide an opportunity for experience at film composing and scoring. Working in school or local musical theater companies can provide valuable experience. Personal connections made in these projects may be very helpful in the professional world that lies ahead. Developing a portfolio of work will be helpful as the composer enters a professional career.

Producers of public service announcements, or PSAs, for radio and television are frequently on the lookout for pro bono (volunteer) work that can provide opportunities for young, willing composers. Such opportunities may be listed in trade magazines, such as *Variety* (available in print or online at http://www.variety.com) and *Show Business* (in print or online at http://showbusinessweekly.com).

Joining the American Federation of Musicians and other musical societies and associations is another good move for aspiring composers. Among the associations that can be contacted are Meet the Composer, the American Composers Alliance, Broadcast Music, Inc., and the American Society of Composers, Authors, and Publishers, all located in New York City. These associations and the trade papers are also good sources for leads on grants and awards for which composers can apply.

Young composers, songwriters, and jingle writers can also work their way into the commercial advertising business, by doing some research and taking entry-level jobs with agencies that handle musical commercials.

Advancement

Moving ahead in the music world is strictly done on an individual basis. There is no hierarchical structure to climb, although in record companies a person with music writing talent might move into a producing or A&R (Artists & Repertoire) job and be able to exercise compositional skills in those capacities. Advancement is based on talent, determination, and, probably, luck. Some composers become well known for their work with film scores, John Williams, of *Star Wars* fame, is one.

Advancement for composers often takes place on a highly personal level. They may progress through their careers to writing music of greater complexity and in more challenging structures. They may develop a unique style, and even develop new forms and traditions of music. One day, their name might be added to the list of the great composers.

Earnings

A few composers make huge annual incomes while many make little or nothing. Some make a very large income in one or two years and none in succeeding years. While many composers receive royalties on repeat performances of their work, most depend on commissions to support themselves. Commissions vary widely according to the type of work and the industry for which the work will be performed. The U.S. Department of Labor reports that the median yearly income for music directors and composers holding salaried positions was $31,510 in 2000. Even for those in salaried positions, however, earnings range widely. The lowest paid 10 percent of this group made less than $13,530 in 2000, while the highest paid 10 percent earned more than $66,140.

Many composers, however, do not hold full-time salaried positions and are only paid in royalties for their compositions that sell. According to the American Society of Composers, Authors, and Publishers (ASCAP), the royalty rate for 2001 was $7.55 per song per album sold. The $7.55 is divided between the composer and the publisher, based on their agreement. After 2001, the composer and publisher will receive an additional $.08 per album sold. Therefore, given these royalty rates, a composer with one song on an album that sold 200,000 copies in 2001 would receive $15,100 to be divided with his or her publisher. If the album sold another 25,000 copies in 2002 the royalties the composer and publisher received would be $2,000. Naturally, if this song is the only one the composer has that brings in income during 2001 and 2002, his or her annual earnings are extremely low (keep in mind that the composer only receives a percentage of the $15,100 and the $2,000).

On the other hand, a composer who creates music for a feature film may have substantial earnings, according to the ASCAP. Factors that influence the composer's earnings include how much music is needed for the film, the film's total budget, if the film will be distributed to a general audience or only have limited showings, and the reputation of the composer. ASCAP notes that depending on such factors, a composer can receive fees ranging from $20,000 for a lower-budget, small film to more than $1,000,000 if the film is a big-budget release from a major studio and the composer is well known.

Many composers must hold a second job in order to make ends meet financially. In some cases these second jobs, such as teaching, will provide benefits such as health insurance and paid vacation time. Composers who work independently, however, need to provide insurance and other benefits for themselves.

Work Environment

The physical conditions of a composer's workplace can vary according to personal taste and what is affordable. Some work in expensive, state-of-the-art home studios, others in a bare room with an electric keyboard or a guitar. An aspiring composer may work in a cramped and cluttered room in a New York City tenement, or a Hollywood ranch home.

For the serious composer the work is likely to be personally rewarding, but financially unrewarding. For the commercial writer, some degree of financial reward is more likely, but competition is fierce, and the big prize goes only to the rarest of individuals. Getting started requires great dedication and sacrifice. Even those protected by academia must give up most of their spare time to composing, often sitting down to the piano when exhausted from a full day of teaching. There are many frustrations along the way. The career composer must learn to live with rejection and have the verve and determination to keep coming back time and again. Under these circumstances, composers can only succeed by having complete faith in their own work.

Outlook

The U.S. Department of Labor, which classifies composers in the category of musicians, singers, and related workers, predicts employment in this field to grow about as fast as the average through 2010. Although there are no reliable statistics on the number of people who make their living solely from composing, the general consensus is that very few people can sustain themselves through composing alone. The field is highly competitive and crowded with highly talented people trying to have their music published and played. There are only a limited number of commissions, grants, and awards available at any time, and the availability of these is often subjected to changes in the economy. On the other hand, many films continue to be made each year, particularly as cable television companies produce more and more original programs. However, the chances of new composers supporting themselves by their music alone will likely always remain rare.

For More Information

For music news, news on legislation affecting musicians, and the magazine International Musician, *contact the following union:*

American Federation of Musicians of the United States and Canada
1501 Broadway, Suite 600
New York, NY 10036
Tel: 212-869-1330
Email: info@afm.org
Web: http://www.afm.org

The ASCAP Web site has industry news, information on workshops and awards, and practical information about the business of music.

American Society of Composers, Authors, and Publishers (ASCAP)
One Lincoln Plaza
New York, NY 10023
Tel: 212-621-6000
Email: info@ascap.com
Web: http://www.ascap.com

This organization represents songwriters, composers, and music publishers. Its Web site has much information on the industry.

Broadcast Music, Inc.
320 West 57th Street
New York, NY 10019-3790
Tel: 212-586-2000
Web: http://www.bmi.com

The Meet the Composer Web site has information on awards and residencies as well as interviews with composers active in the field today.

Meet the Composer
2112 Broadway, Suite 505
New York, NY 10023
Tel: 212-787-3601
Web: http://www.meetthecomposer.org

At select cities, SGA offers song critiques and other workshops. Visit its Web site for further information on such events.

Songwriters Guild of America (SGA)
National Projects Office
1560 Broadway, Suite 1306
New York, NY 10036
Tel: 212-768-7902
Web: http://www.songwriters.org

Dancers and Choreographers

	School Subjects
Music	
Theater/dance	

	Personal Skills
Artistic	
Communication/ideas	

	Work Environment
Primarily indoors	
Primarily multiple locations	

	Minimum Education Level
High school diploma	

	Salary Range
$12,520 to $22,470 to $55,800+	

	Certification or Licensing
None available	

	Outlook
About as fast as the average	

Overview

Dancers perform dances alone or with others. Through dancing, they attempt to tell a story, interpret an idea, or simply express rhythm and sound by supplying preconceived physical movements to music. *Choreographers* create or develop dance patterns and teach them to performers. Professional dancers and choreographers often have periods of unemployment in the field as they move from project to project. At any one time, there are approximately 26,000 dancers and choreographers working in the United States.

History

Dancing is one of the oldest of the arts. The first formal dances were the ritualistic, symbolic dances of early tribal societies: the dance designed to excite the emotions, such as the war dance; the dance purporting to communicate with the gods, such as the rain dance. Dances are an important part of any culture. In the United States, for example, the square dance became a part of our folkways. Dancing has become a popular leisure-time activity, a popular form of entertainment, and, for those who provide the entertainment, a career. There are many types of dancing, from ballet to tap dancing, jazz and modern dance, and ballroom dancing.

Ballet has its origins in Italy and France in the 15th centuries, when dance was used to help orchestrate a story around a celebration. The early Italian balletto combined dance, poetry, song, and elaborate scenery, and a performance could last for hours or days. The balletto was brought to France by Catherine de Medici (1519-89), married to the French king Henry II in 1533, where it was renamed ballet. In the next century King Louis XIV founded L'Academie Royale de Danse, where, under dancing master Pierre Beauchamps, the classical ballet positions were first codified. By the end of the 17th century, the French terms had become the international language of ballet. It was not until the beginning of the 18th century, however, that ballet became a profession, with its own schools, theaters, paid dancers, and choreographers. As ballet grew, choreographers and dancers developed new ideas, movements, and ideas, and composers began creating music especially for ballet. Noted choreographers and dancers were Jean Philippe Rameau, Franz Hiverding, Jean Georges Noverre, and August Vetris. In the late 18th and early 19th centuries, choreographers were creating ballets that are still performed today. One of the oldest of such ballets is the French La Fille Mal Gardee choreographed by Jean Dauberval. Pointe shoes, and the style of dancing on the toes, were developed toward the middle of the 19th century. The end of the 19th century saw the creation of many famous ballets, still among the most popular in the world today, including *The Nutcracker Suite, Sleeping Beauty,* and *Swan Lake.*

Modern dance is a distinct art form of the 20th century. Unlike ballet, modern dance has no set forms or techniques, and is oriented more toward individual expression in its choreography. Rather than presenting an interpretation of a story or narrative, modern dance expresses such abstract concepts as time, space, emotion, or pure movement. The pioneer of modern dance was Isadora Duncan, who introduced the form around the turn of the century. Duncan's lead was followed in 1915 by the creation of the Denishawn School in Los Angeles, considered to be the founder of the modern dance movement. Several dancers from this school went on to form their own schools, including Doris Humphrey and Charles Weidman, and Martha Graham. In the 1930s, Lester Horton and Helen Tamiris gave rise to another current of modern dance, which went on to inspire the works of Merce Cunningham, Alvin Ailey, Twyla Tharp, and others.

Tap dancing originated from early Irish and English folk dances, as well as in the African dances brought to the United States by the African slaves. Wearing shoes with metal strips fitted to the heels and toes, tap dancers create often complex rhythms by striking their heels and toes on the floor. Developed through minstrel shows, and later through vaudeville, musicals, and film, tap dancing soon became a popular form of entertainment. The first choreographed tap dancing routines were performed by the Floradora Sextet in 1900. Later popularizers of tap dancing included Bill "Bojangles" Robinson, Fred Astaire, and Ruby Keeler, and, in more recent years, Gregory Hines.

In addition to many traditional folk and ethnic dances, many other dances have developed through the years, including popular ballroom dances such as swing, the fox trot, the tango, the mambo, the cha cha, and others, and more recently popular dances such as salsa, the merengue, and hip-hop.

The Job

Dancers usually dance together as a chorus. As they advance in their profession, dancers may do special numbers with other selected dancers and, when a reputation is attained, the dancer may do solo work. The following are five popular forms of dancing, and although some dancers become proficient in all four, most dancers attempt to specialize in one specific area.

The *acrobatic dancer* performs a style of dancing characterized by difficult gymnastic feats.

The *ballet dancer* performs artistic dances suggesting a theme or story. Ballet is perhaps one of the most exacting and demanding forms of dance. Most other types of dancers need some type of ballet training.

The *interpretive* or *modern dancer* performs dances that interpret moods or characterizations. Facial expression and the body are used to express the theme of the dance.

The *tap dancer* performs a style of dancing that is distinguished by rhythm tapped by the feet in time with the music.

Ballroom dancers perform social dances such as the waltz, fox trot, cha-cha, tango, and rhumba.

In all dancing, grace and execution are basic. Some dances require specific traditional movements and precise positions. Others provide for planned movement but permit sufficient variation in execution. The dancer thus is able to include a spin, a dip, a pause, or some other effect that provides a certain amount of individuality and flair to the performance.

Dancing is a profession that permits the performers to make the most of their physical features and personality. Part of the success of dancers depends on the ability to use their assets in ways that will permit their full expression.

Dancers may perform in classical ballet or modern dance, in dance adaptations for musical shows, in folk dances, or in tap and other types of popular dancing productions. Some dancers compete in contests for specific types of dancing such as ballroom dancing.

A few dancers have become choreographers, who create new ballets or dance routines. They must be knowledgeable about dancing, music, costume, lighting, and dramatics. Others are dance directors and train the dancers in productions. Many dancers combine teaching with their stage work or are full-time dance instructors in ballet schools or in colleges and universities. Some open their own dancing schools with specialties such as ballet for children or ballroom dancing.

A small number of dancers and choreographers work in music videos. While they may not become rich or famous in this line of work, it does provide good experience and increases their visibility.

Requirements

High School

A good high school education is highly recommended for those interested in becoming dancers. You should take courses in speech, music, and dramatics, and engage in extracurricular activities that will enhance your knowledge of these areas. You should also continue your dance studies during the summer. Some summer camps feature dance training, and special summer classes are available in some large cities.

Postsecondary Training

A number of avenues for advanced training are available. About 240 colleges and universities offer programs leading to a bachelor's or higher degree in dance, generally through the departments of physical education, music, theater, or fine arts. These programs provide an opportunity for a college education and advanced preparation and training. Other possibilities include study with professional dancing teachers or attendance at a professional dance school. There are a number of such schools in the country; most of them are located in large cities.

Experience as a performer is usually required for teaching in professional schools, and graduate degrees are generally required by colleges and conservatories.

Other Requirements

There are no formal educational requirements, but an early start (around eight for ballet) and years of practice are basic to a successful career. The preparation for a professional dancing career is as much a test of your personal characteristics as it is of your talent. You need, first and foremost, to be enthusiastic about dancing, for the basic desire to achieve success is an ingredient that will help you overcome some of the disappointment and setbacks that seem to be hurdles normally encountered.

The physical demands of daily practice as well as the demands of the dance routine necessitate good health and a strong body. A dancer must also have a feeling for music, a sense of rhythm, and grace and agility. Good feet with normal arches are required. Persistence and sensitivity, as they apply to the day-to-day preparation of the dancer, are also important personal characteristics.

Exploring

Dancing is a highly competitive profession, and you should take advantage of every opportunity to gain experience and increase your skills. Naturally, you should be taking dance lessons, and usually this will also give you the opportunity to perform publicly. Try to get as much experience as you can performing publicly as both a solo dancer and with groups.

Your dance instructor is also a valuable source of information regarding this career. If you are interested in choreography, your instructor may allow you to work up routines to perform. Instructors can also speak from personal experience about the dance schools they attended as well as give advice about what schools they think might be right for you. If you are located near colleges or universities that offer dance programs, make an appointment to visit the department and talk to a student or faculty member there. This will increase your knowledge of what programs are available and what their requirements are.

Finally, use your library, a bookstore, or the Internet to find and read articles about dance, choreography, and happenings in the dance world. One publication to look for, for example, is *Dance Magazine* (http://www.dancemagazine.com), which contains useful information for young dancers.

Employers

Dancers and choreographers are employed by dance companies, opera companies, theater companies, and film and video companies. They are also hired for individual shows and performances that may run anywhere from one night only to several years. Most opportunities are located in major metropolitan areas, New York City being the primary center of dance in the United States. Other cities that have full-time dance companies include San Francisco, Chicago, Boston, Philadelphia, Pittsburgh, Miami, and Washington, DC. Many smaller cities also have their own resident dance and theater companies. After several years of experience, dancers and choreographers often start their own companies based in studios that also may offer classes to both professionals and amateurs.

Dancers and choreographers who are interested in teaching may find employment in high school and postsecondary schools. Teaching opportunities are also available in local dance studios that offer classes to age groups that vary from preschool to adult. Other employers might include local park districts, senior citizens homes, youth centers, and social service agencies like the YMCA.

Starting Out

The only way to get started in dancing is to dance, to take advantage of every performance opportunity possible. Local groups are usually in the market for entertainment at their meetings or social affairs. These appearances provide the opportunity to polish routines and develop the professional air that distinguishes the professional from the amateur performer. Breaking the professional barrier by achieving one's first paid performance can be accomplished in several ways. Take advantage of every audition. Follow the announcements in the trade magazines. Circulate among other dancers. Attend shows and get to know everyone who may be in a position to help with a job.

Another possibility that should be considered is to register with recognized booking agents.

Advancement

As in all performing arts, the star on the dressing room door is the dream of dancing aspirants. Yet top billing, a name in lights, or being the program headliner are positions of accomplishment reserved for a very small number. Many dancers start by earning a spot in the dancing chorus of an off-Broadway musical, in the line at a supper club, or in a dancing group on a television variety show or spectacular. Such opportunities permit further study and lessons, yet enable one to work with experienced choreographers and producers. Earning a spot as a chorus dancer in television on a regular weekly show could provide as many as 13, 26, or 39 performances with the same group.

In recent years, a number of musical stock companies have originated throughout the United States, thus providing another avenue for employment. Although many of these operate only in summer, they provide experience of a Broadway nature. Outdoor spectaculars such as exhibitions, parades, fairs, and festivals often use dance acts.

Working on the road can be an exciting, yet tiring, opportunity. Chorus groups with traveling musicals and cafe shows provide regular employment for a season. The numbers are rehearsed before the tour and very little adaptation or change is possible. One does get a chance to perform in a variety of situations and with different bands or orchestras because accompaniments are different in each club or community performance.

Dancers may also advance to choreographing, one of the most creative and responsible jobs in dancing. Other dancers find positions as teachers and some eventually open their own schools.

Dancers join various unions depending on the type of dance they perform. The American Guild of Musical Artists is the union to which dancers belong who perform in opera ballets, classical ballet, and modern dance. Those on live or taped television join the American Federation of Television and Radio Artists. Dancers in films have the Screen Actors Guild or the Screen Extras Guild. Those who appear on stage in musical comedies join the Actors' Equity Association. And those who dance in nightclubs and variety shows belong to the American Guild of Variety Artists.

Earnings

Dancers' yearly earnings vary widely depending on factors such as where a dancer is employed, how much work he or she was able to get for the year, and what role the dancer performed in a production. The U.S. Department of Labor reports that the median annual income for dancers was $22,470 in 2000. The lowest paid 10 percent of dancers earned less than $12,520 that same period; while the highest paid 10 percent made more than $55,220. Dancers on tour usually receive additional money to use for room and food and may also get extra money for overtime.

Because of the lack of steady, well-paying work, many dancers must supplement their income with earnings from other jobs. Possibilities include teaching dance, working several part-time dance jobs, or going outside the field for other work.

According to the U.S. Department of Labor, choreographers had the median yearly income of $27,010 in 2000. Like dancers' incomes, choreographers' earnings vary widely. The lowest paid 10 percent of choreographers made less than $13,370 in 2000; while at the other end of the pay scale, the highest paid 10 percent earned more than $55,800.

Many dancers and choreographers belong to unions, and those working under union contracts may receive some benefits such as health insurance and paid sick leave. Those who do not work under union contracts typically receive no benefits and must provide for their own health insurance, retirement plans, and other benefits.

Work Environment

The irregularity of employment is the most difficult aspect of the profession. Dancers are never certain where they will be employed or under what conditions. One may wait weeks for a contract. An offer may involve travel, night hours, or weekend rehearsals. Work on a Broadway stage show may last 20 weeks, 40 weeks, or three years, or possibly the show will fold after the third performance. With rehearsals and performances, a normal work week runs 30 hours (six hours a day maximum).

Dancing requires considerable sacrifices of both a personal and social nature. Dancing is the performing dancer's life. The demands of practice and the need to continue lessons and to learn new routines and variations leave little time for recreational or social activities. As a career, dancing necessitates greater emphasis on self than on others; the intensive competition and the need to project oneself to get ahead leave little time for other pursuits.

Outlook

Employment of dancers is expected to increase about as fast as the national occupational average through the next decade, but those seeking a career in dancing will find the field highly competitive and uncertain. For performers, there are limited opportunities since there are more trained dancers than job openings. Television has provided additional positions, but the number of stage and screen productions is declining. The best opportunities may exist in regional ballet companies, opera companies, and dance groups affiliated with colleges and universities. The turnover rate in dancing is rather high so there are always openings for the newcomer. Although generalization is difficult, the average chorus dancer can expect a career of five to 10 years at best. Most ballet dancers stop dancing for an audience before they are 40 years of age.

The dancer who can move from performing to teaching will find other employment possibilities in colleges, universities, and schools of dance; with civic and community groups; and in the operation of dance studios.

For More Information

This is a union for singers, dancers, and other performers in operas and other classical music productions and concerts. The Web site has information on auditions, legal actions against employers, and union news.

American Guild of Musical Artists
1727 Broadway at 55th Street
New York, NY 10019
Tel: 212-265-3687
Web: http://www.musicalartists.org

Visit Dance Magazine's *Web site to read abstracts of articles that appear in the print version. For general questions, contact:*

Dance Magazine
111 Myrtle Street, Suite 203
Oakland, CA 94607
Tel: 510-839-6060
Web: http://www.dancemagazine.com

A directory of dance companies and related organizations and other information on professional dance is available from Dance/USA. Visit the Young Dancer Information link on its Web site for helpful news and advice.

Dance/USA
1156 15th Street, NW, Suite 820
Washington, DC 20005
Tel: 202-833-1717
Web: http://www.danceusa.org

A directory of accredited programs is available from NASD. Approved member institutions can also be found listed on its Web site, which also contains a help-ful FAQ section for students.

National Association of Schools of Dance (NASD)
11250 Roger Beacon Drive, Suite 21
Reston, VA 22090
Tel: 703-437-0700
Email: info@arts-accredit.org
Web: http://www.arts-accredit.org

NDA compiles a dance directory with information on universities, colleges, dance studios, and high schools that offer dance education and programs. Visit its Web site for more information on the directory and scholarships and awards.

National Dance Association (NDA)
1900 Association Drive
Reston, VA 20191
Tel: 703-476-3421
Email: nda@aahperd.org
Web: http://www.aahperd.org/nda

Disc Jockeys

Overview

Disc jockeys play recorded music on radio or during parties, dances, and special events. On the radio they intersperse the music with a variety of advertising material and informal commentary. They may also perform such public services as announcing the time, the weather forecast, or important news. Interviewing guests and making public service announcements may also be part of the disc jockey's work. There are about 50,000 disc jockeys in the United States.

History

Guglielmo Marconi (1874-1937), a young Italian engineer, first transmitted a radio signal in his home in 1895. Radio developed rapidly as people began to comprehend its tremendous possibilities. The stations KDKA in Pittsburgh and WWWJ in Detroit began broadcasting in 1920. Within 10 years, there were radio stations in all the major cities in the United States and broadcasting had become big business. The National Broadcasting Company became the first network in 1926 when it linked together 25 stations across the country. The Columbia Broadcasting System was organized the following year. In 1934, the Mutual Broadcasting Company was founded. The years between 1930 and 1950 may be considered the zenith years for the radio industry. With the coming of television, radio broadcasting took second place in importance as entertainment for the home, but radio's commercial and communications value should not be underestimated.

The first major contemporary disc jockey in the United States was Alan Freed (1921-65), who worked in the 1950s on WINS radio in New York. In 1957, his rock and roll stage shows at the Paramount Theater made front-page news in *The New York Times* because of the huge crowds they attracted. The title "disc jockey" arose when most music was recorded on conventional flat records or discs.

Today, much of the recorded music used in commercial radio stations is on magnetic tape or compact disc. The disc jockey personalities are still very much a part of the radio station's image, with major players commanding salaries at the top of the range.

The Job

Disc jockeys serve as a bridge between the music itself and the listener. They also perform such public services as announcing the time, the weather forecast, or important news. Working at a radio station can be a lonely job, since often the disc jockey is the only person in the studio. But because their job is to maintain the good spirits of their audience and attract new listeners, disc jockeys must possess the ability to sound relaxed and cheerful.

Dave Wineland is a disc jockey at WRZQ 107.3 in Columbus, Indiana. He covers the popular 5:30 to 10 AM morning shift that many commuters listen to on their way to work. Like many disc jockeys, his duties extend beyond on-the-air announcements. He works as production director at the station and writes and produces many of the commercials and promotion announcements. "I spend a lot of time in the production room," says Wineland, who also delegates some of the production duties to other disc jockeys on the staff.

Unlike the more conventional radio or television announcer, the disc jockey is not bound by a written script. Except for the commercial announcements, which must be read as written, the disc jockey's statements are usually spontaneous. Disc jockeys are not usually required to play a musical selection to the end; they may fade out a record when it interferes with a predetermined schedule for commercials, news, time checks, or weather reports. Disc jockeys are not always free to play what they want; at some radio stations, especially the larger ones, the program director or the music director makes the decisions about the music that will be played. And while some stations may encourage their disc jockeys to talk, others emphasize music over commentary and restrict the amount of a DJ's ad-libbing.

Disc jockeys should be levelheaded and able to react calmly even in the face of a crisis. Many unexpected circumstances can arise that demand the skill of quick thinking. For example, if guests who are to appear on a program either do not arrive or become too nervous to go on the air, the disc jockey must fill the airtime. He or she must also smooth over a breakdown in equipment or some other technical difficulty.

Many disc jockeys have become well-known public personalities in broadcasting; they may participate in community activities and public events.

Disc jockeys who work at parties and other special events usually work on a part-time basis. They are often called party DJs. A DJ who works for a supplying company receives training, equipment, music, and job assignments from the company. Self-employed DJs must provide everything they need themselves. Party DJs have more contact with people than radio DJs, so they must be personable and patient with clients.

Requirements

High School

In high school, you can start to prepare for a career as a disc jockey. A good knowledge of the English language, correct pronunciation, and diction are important. High school English classes as well as speech classes are helpful in getting a good familiarity with the language. Extracurricular activities such as debating and theater will also help with learning good pronunciation and projection.

Many high schools have radio stations on site where students can work as disc jockeys, production managers, or technicians. This experience can be a good starting point to learn more about the field. Dave Wineland's first radio job was at the radio station at Carmel High School in Indianapolis.

Postsecondary Training

Although there are no formal educational requirements for becoming a disc jockey, many large stations prefer applicants with some college education. Some schools train students for broadcasting, but such training will not necessarily improve the chances of an applicant's getting a job at a radio station.

Students interested in becoming a disc jockey and advancing to other broadcasting positions should attend a school that will train them to become an announcer. There are some private broadcasting schools that offer good courses, but others are poor; students should get references from the school or the local Better Business Bureau before taking classes.

Like many disc jockeys today, Wineland has a college degree. He earned a degree in telecommunications from Ball State University.

Candidates may also apply for any job at a radio station and work their way up. Competition for disc jockey positions is strong. Although there may not be any specific training program required by prospective employers, station officials pay particular attention to taped auditions of the applicant. Companies that hire DJs for parties will often train them; experience is not always necessary if the applicant has a suitable personality.

Other Requirements

Union membership may be required for employment with large stations in major cities and is a necessity with the networks. The largest talent union is the American Federation of Television and Radio Artists. Most small stations, however, are nonunion.

Exploring

If becoming a disc jockey sounds interesting, you might try to get a summer job at a radio station. Although you will probably not have any opportunity to broadcast, you may be able to judge whether or not that kind of work appeals to you as a career.

Take advantage of any opportunity you get to speak or perform before an audience. Appearing as a speaker or a performer can help you decide whether or not you have the necessary stage presence for a career on the air.

Many colleges and universities have their own radio stations and offer courses in radio. Students gain valuable experience working at college-owned stations. Some radio stations offer students financial assistance and on-the-job training in the form of internships and co-op work programs, as well as scholarships and fellowships.

Employers

There has been a steady growth in the number of radio stations in the United States. According to 2001 statistics from the National Association of Broadcasters, the United States alone has 12,932 radio stations.

Radio is a 24-hour-a-day, seven-day-a-week medium, so there are many slots to fill. Most of these stations are small stations where disc jockeys are required to perform many other duties for a lower salary than at larger stations in bigger metropolitan areas.

Due to the Telecommunications Act of 1996, companies can own an unlimited number of radio stations nationwide with an eight-station limit within one market area, depending on the size of the market. When this legislation took effect, mergers and acquisitions changed the face of the radio industry. So, while the pool of employers is smaller, the number of stations continues to rise.

Starting Out

One way to enter this field is to apply for an entry-level job rather than a job as a disc jockey. It is also advisable to start at a small local station. As opportunities arise, DJs commonly move from one station to another.

While still a high school student, Dave Wineland applied for a position at his local radio station in Monticello, Indiana. "I was willing to work long hours for low pay," he says, acknowledging that starting out in radio can require some sacrifices. However, on-air experience is a must.

An announcer is employed only after an audition. Audition material should be selected carefully to show the prospective employer the range of the applicant's abilities. A prospective DJ should practice talking aloud, alone, then make a tape of him- or herself with five to seven minutes of material to send to radio stations. The tape should include a news story, two 60-second commercials, and a sample of the applicant introducing and coming out of a record. (Tapes should not include the whole song, just the first and final few seconds, with the aspiring DJ introducing and finishing the music; this is called "telescoping.") In addition to presenting prepared materials, applicants may also be asked to read material that they have not seen previously. This may be a commercial, news release, dramatic selection, or poem.

Advancement

Most successful disc jockeys advance from small stations to large ones. The typical experienced disc jockey will have held several jobs at different stations.

Some careers lead from being a disc jockey to other types of radio or television work. More people are employed in sales, promotion, and planning than in performing, and they are often paid more than disc jockeys.

Earnings

The salary range for disc jockeys is extremely broad with a low of $7,000 and a high of $100,000. The average salary in the late 1990s was $31,251, according to a survey conducted by the National Association of Broadcasters (NAB) and the Broadcast Cable Financial Management Association.

Smaller market areas and smaller stations fall closer to the bottom of the range, while the top markets and top-rated stations offer disc jockeys higher salaries. In large markets such as Chicago, earnings can range depending on broadcast time. According to a survey by the accounting and consulting firm of Hungerford, Aldrin, Nichols and Carter, morning radio announcers made as much as $160,000 in 1999. Those that work later in the day earn considerably less. Afternoon announcers made an average of $80,000 a year, and evening announcers earned closer to $60,000. In the same report, overnight and weekend disc jockeys earned $40,000 and $27,000, respectively.

Benefits for disc jockeys vary according to the size of the market and station. However, vacation and sick time is somewhat limited because the medium requires that radio personalities be on the air nearly every day.

Work Environment

Work in radio stations is usually very pleasant. Almost all stations are housed in modern facilities. Temperature and dust control are important factors in the proper maintenance of technical electronic equipment, and people who work around such machinery benefit from the precautions taken to preserve it.

The work can be demanding. It requires that every activity or comment on the air begin and end exactly on time. This can be difficult, especially when the disc jockey has to handle news, commercials, music, weather, and guests within a certain time frame. It takes a lot of skill to work the controls, watch the clock, select music, talk with a caller or guest, read reports, and entertain the audience; often several of these tasks must be performed simultaneously. A disc jockey must be able to plan ahead and stay alert so that when one song ends he or she is ready with the next song or with a scheduled commercial.

Because radio audiences listen to disc jockeys who play the music they like and talk about the things that interest them, disc jockeys must always be aware of pleasing their audience. If listeners begin switching stations, ratings go down and disc jockeys can lose their jobs.

Disc jockeys do not always have job security; if the owner or manager of a radio station changes, the disc jockey may lose his or her job. The consolidation of radio stations to form larger, cost-efficient stations has caused some employees to lose their jobs.

Disc jockeys usually work a 40-hour week, but they may work irregular hours. They may have to report for work at a very early hour in the morning. Sometimes they will be free during the daytime hours, but will have to work late into the night. Some radio stations operate on a 24-hour basis. All-night announcers may be alone in the station during their working hours.

The disc jockey who stays with a station for a period of time becomes a well-known personality in the community. Such celebrities are sought after as participants in community activities and may be recognized on the street.

Disc jockeys who work at parties and other events work in a variety of settings. They generally have more freedom to choose music selections but little opportunity to ad-lib. Their work is primarily on evenings and weekends.

Outlook

According to the National Association of Broadcasters, radio reaches 77 percent of people over the age of 12 everyday. Despite radio's popularity, the *Occupational Outlook Handbook* projects that employment of announcers will decline slightly through 2010. Due to this decline, competition for jobs will be great in an already competitive field.

While small stations will still hire beginners, on-air experience will be increasingly important. Another area where job seekers can push ahead of the competition is in specialization. Knowledge of specific areas such as business, consumer, and health news may be advantageous.

While on-air radio personalities are not necessarily affected by economic downturns, mergers and changes in the industry can affect employment. If a radio station has to make cuts due to the economy, it is most likely to do so in the behind-the-scenes area, which means that the disc jockeys who remain may face a further diversity in their duties.

For More Information

For a list of schools offering degrees in broadcasting as well as scholarship information, contact:

Broadcast Education Association
1771 N Street, NW
Washington, DC 20036-2891
Tel: 202-429-5354
Web: http://www.beaweb.org

For broadcast education, support, and scholarship information, contact:

National Association of Broadcasters
1771 N Street, NW
Washington, DC 20036
Tel: 202-429-5300
Email: nab@nab.org
Web: http://www.nab.org

For college programs and union information, contact:

National Association of Broadcast Employees and Technicians
501 Third Street, NW, 8th Floor
Washington, DC 20001
Tel: 202-434-1254
Web: http://nabetcwa.org

For scholarship and internship information, contact:

Radio-Television News Directors Association and Foundation
1600 K Street, NW, Suite 700
Washington, DC 20006-2838
Tel: 202-659-6510
Web: http://www.rtnda.org

Film and Television Directors

	School Subjects
English	
Theater/dance	
	Personal Skills
Artistic	
Leadership/management	
	Work Environment
Indoors and outdoors	
Primarily multiple locations	
	Minimum Education Level
Bachelor's degree	
	Salary Range
$20,000 to $50,000 to $500,000+	
	Certification or Licensing
None available	
	Outlook
Faster than the average	

Overview

"Lights! Camera! Action!" aptly summarizes the major responsibilities of the *film and television director*. In ultimate control of the decisions that shape a film or television production, the director is an artist who coordinates the elements of a film or television show and is responsible for its overall style and quality.

Directors are well known for their part in guiding actors, but they are involved in much more—casting, costuming, cinematography, editing, and sound recording. Directors must have insight into the many tasks that go into the creation of a film, and they must have a broad vision of how each part will contribute to the big picture.

History

The playwrights and actors of ancient Greece were tellers of tales, striving to impress and influence audiences with their dramatic interpretations of stories. That tradition continues today on stages and film screens throughout the world.

From the days of the Greek theater until sometime in the 19th century, actors directed themselves. Although modern motion picture directors can find their roots in the theater, it was not until the mid-1880s that the director became someone other than a member of the acting cast. It had been common practice for one of the actors involved in a production to be responsible not only for his or her own performance but also for conducting rehearsals and coordinating the tasks involved in putting on a play. Usually the most experienced and respected troupe member would guide the other actors, providing advice on speech, movement, and interaction.

A British actress and opera singer named Madame Vestris (1797-1856) is considered to have been the first professional director. In the 1830s Vestris leased a theater in London and staged productions in which she herself did not perform. She displayed a new, creative approach to directing, making bold decisions about changing the traditional dress code for actors and allowing them to express their own interpretations of their roles. Vestris coordinated rehearsals, advised on lighting and sound effects, and chose nontraditional set decorations; she introduced props, such as actual windows and doors, that were more realistic than the usual painted panoramas.

By the turn of the century, theater directors such as David Belasco (1859-1931) and Konstantin Stanislavsky (1863-1938) had influenced the way in which performances were given, provoking actors and actresses to strive to identify with the characters they revealed so that audiences would be passionately and genuinely affected. By the early 1900s, Stanislavsky's method of directing performers had made an overwhelming mark on drama. His method (now often referred to as "the Method"), as well as his famous criticism, "I do not believe you," continue to influence performers to this day.

At this same time, the motion picture industry was coming into being. European filmmakers such as Leon Gaumont (1864-1946), and New Yorker Edwin S. Porter (1870-1941), were directing, filming, and producing minutes-long pictures. The industry's first professional female director was Alice Guy, who worked with Gaumont in the early years of the 20th century. The technical sophistication offered by today's professionals was not part of the early directors' repertoire. They merely filmed narratives without moving their camera. Soon directors began to experiment, moving the camera to shoot various angles and establishing a variety of editing techniques.

By 1915 there were close to 20,000 movie theaters in the United States; by the early 1920s, 40 million people were going to Hollywood-produced and -directed silent movies every week. Successful actors such as Charlie Chaplin and Buster Keaton began directing their own films, and Frank Capra and Cecil B. De Mille were starting their long careers as professional directors.

With the emergence of "talking pictures" in the early 1930s, the director's role changed significantly. Sound in film provided opportunities for further directorial creativity. Unnecessary noise could not be tolerated on the set; directors had to be concerned with the voices of their performers and the potential sound effects that could be created. Directors could demand certain types of voices (e.g., a Southern drawl) and sound effects (e.g., the rat-a-tat-tat of submachine guns) to present accurate interpretations of scripts. And no longer was the visually funny slapstick humor enough to make viewers laugh. Much of the humor in sound comedies arose from the script and from the successful direction of professionals like Frank Capra and Ernst Lubitsch (1892-1947).

The U.S. film industry experienced crises and controversy during the next 50 years, including financial problems, conglomerations of studios, and the introduction of the ratings system. New genres and elements began to challenge directorial genius over the years: science fiction, adventure, film noir; graphic representation of violence and sex; and sensational and computer-enhanced special effects. By the 1970s, university film schools had been established and were sending out creative directors such as Francis Ford Coppola, George Lucas, Martin Scorsese, and Steven Spielberg, to name a few. Hollywood was reborn with the technical sophistication understood by these directors.

The Job

Film directors, also called *filmmakers,* are considered to bear ultimate responsibility for the tone and quality of the films they work on. They interpret the stories and narratives presented in scripts and coordinate the filming of their interpretations. They are involved in preproduction, production, and postproduction. They audition, select, and rehearse the acting crew; they work on matters regarding set designs, musical scores, and costumes; and they decide on details such as where scenes should be shot, what backgrounds might be needed, and how special effects could be employed.

The director of a film often works with a *casting director,* who is in charge of auditioning performers. The casting director pays close attention to attributes of the performers such as physical appearance, quality of voice, and acting ability and experience, and then presents to the director a list of suitable candidates for each role.

One of the most important aspects of the film director's job is working with the performers. Directors have their own styles of extracting accurate emotion and performance from cast members, but they must be dedicated to this goal.

Two common techniques that categorize directors' styles are montage and mise-en-scene. *Montage directors* are concerned with using editing techniques to produce desired results; they consider it important to focus on how individual shots will work when pieced together with others. Consider Alfred Hitchcock (1899-1980), who directed the production of one scene in *Psycho,* for example, by filming discrete shots in a bathroom and then editing in dialogue, sound effects, and music to create tremendous suspense. *Mise-en-scene directors* are more concerned with the pre-editing phase, focusing on the elements of angles, movement, and design one shot at a time, as Orson Welles (1915-85) did. Many directors combine elements of both techniques in their work.

The film's *art director* creates set design concepts and chooses shoot locations. He or she meets with the filmmaker and producer to set budgets and schedules and then accordingly coordinates the construction of sets. Research is done on the period in which the film is to take place, and experts are consulted to help create appropriate architectural and environmental styles. The art director also is often involved in design ideas for costumes, makeup and hairstyles, photographic effects, and other elements of the film's production.

The *director of photography,* or *cinematographer,* is responsible for organizing and implementing the actual camera work. Together with the filmmaker, he or she interprets scenes and decides on appropriate camera motion to achieve desired results. The director of photography determines the amounts of natural and artificial lighting required for each shoot and such technical factors as the type of film to be used, camera angles and distance, depth of field, and focus.

Motion pictures are usually filmed out of sequence, meaning that the ending might be shot first and scenes from the middle of the story might not be filmed until the end of production. Directors are responsible for scheduling each day's sequence of scenes; they coordinate filming so that scenes using the same set and performers will be filmed together. In addition to conferring with the art director and the director of photography, filmmakers meet with technicians and crew members to advise on and approve final scenery, lighting, props, and other necessary equipment. They are also involved with final approval of costumes, choreography, and music.

After all the scenes have been shot, postproduction begins. The director works with picture and sound editors to cut apart and piece together the final reels. The *film editor* shares the director's vision about the picture and assembles shots according to that overall idea, synchronizing film with voice and sound tracks produced by the *sound editor* and *music editor*.

While the director supervises all major aspects of film production, various assistants help throughout the process. In a less creative position than the filmmaker, the *first assistant director* organizes various practical matters involved during the shooting of each scene. The *second assistant director* is a coordinator who works as a liaison among the production office, the first assistant director, and the performers. The *second unit director* coordinates sequences such as scenic inserts and action shots that do not involve the main acting crew.

Requirements

High School

Film and television directors' careers are rather nontraditional. There is no standard training outline involved, no normal progression up a movie industry ladder leading to the director's job. At the very least, a high school diploma, while not technically required if you wish to become a director, will still probably be indispensable to you in terms of the background and education it signifies. As is true of all artists, especially those in a medium as widely disseminated as film, you will need to have rich and varied experience in order to create works that are intelligently crafted and speak to people of many different backgrounds. In high school, courses in English, art, theater, and history will give you a good foundation. Further, a high school diploma will be necessary if you decide to go on to film school. Be active in school and community drama productions, whether as performer, set designer, or cue-card holder.

Postsecondary Training

In college and afterward, take film classes and volunteer to work on other students' films. Dedication, talent, and experience have always been indispensable to a director. No doubt it is beneficial to become aware of one's passion for film as early as possible. Woody Allen, for example, recognized early in his life the importance motion pictures held for him, but he worked as a magician, jazz clarinet player, joke writer, and stand-up comic before ever directing films. Allen took few film courses in his life.

On the other hand, many successful directors such as Francis Ford Coppola and Martha Coolidge have taken the formal film school route. There are more than five hundred film studies programs offered by schools of higher education throughout the United States, including those considered to be the five most reputable: those of the American Film Institute in Los Angeles, Columbia University in New York City, New York University (NYU), the University of California at Los Angeles (UCLA), and the University of Southern California (USC). These schools have film professionals on their faculties and provide a very visible stage for student talent, being located in the two film-business hot spots, California and New York. (The tuition for film programs offered elsewhere, however, tends to be much less expensive than at these schools.)

Film school offers overall formal training, providing an education in fundamental directing skills by working with student productions. Such education is rigorous, but in addition to teaching skills it provides aspiring directors with peer groups and a network of contacts with students, faculty, and guest speakers that can be of help after graduation.

The debate continues on what is more influential in a directing career: film school or personal experience. Some say that it is always possible for creative people to land directing jobs without having gone through a formal program. Competition is so pervasive in the industry that even film school graduates find jobs scarce (only 5 to 10 percent of the 26,000 students who graduate from film schools each year find jobs in the industry). Martha Coolidge, for instance, made independent films for 10 years before directing a Hollywood movie.

Other Requirements

Konstantin Stanislavsky had a passion for his directorial work in the theater, believing that it was an art of immense social importance. Today's motion picture directors must have similar inspiration and possibly even greater creative strength, because of the many more responsibilities involved in directing modern film.

Exploring

If you are a would-be director, the most obvious opportunity for exploration lies in your own imagination. Being drawn to films and captivated by the process of how they are made is the beginning of the filmmaker's journey.

In high school and beyond, pay attention to motion pictures. Watch them at every opportunity, both at the theater and at home. Study your favorite television shows to see what makes them interesting. Two major trade publications to read are *Variety* (http://www.variety.com) and *Hollywood Reporter* (http://www.hollywoodreporter.com). Also, the book *How to Make It in Hollywood: All the Right Moves* (Linda Buzzell, 1996, Harper Perennial) is a very good informal guide that presents insider tips on such factors as "schmoozing" and chutzpah (self-confidence) as well as an extensive list of valuable resources.

During summers, many camps and workshops offer programs for high school students interested in film work. For example, UCLA presents its Media Workshops for students aged 14 to 24. Classes there focus on mass media production, including film, TV, and video. For information, contact the Media Workshops Foundation, Tel: 800-223-4561, Web: http://www.mediaworkshops.org/foundation.

Employers

Employment as a film or television director is usually on a freelance or contractual basis. Directors find work, for example, with film studios (both major and independent), at television stations and cable networks, through advertising agencies, with record companies, and through the creation of their own independent film projects.

Starting Out

It is considered difficult to begin as a motion picture director. With nontraditional steps to professional status, the occupation poses challenges for those seeking employment. However, there is somewhat solid advice for those who wish to direct motion pictures.

Many current directors began their careers in other film industry professions, such as acting or writing. Consider Jodie Foster, who appeared in 30 films and dozens of television productions before she went on to direct her first motion picture at the age of 28. Obviously it helps to grow up near the heart of "Tinseltown" and to have the influence of one's family spurring you on. The support of family and friends is often cited as an essential element in shaping the confidence you need to succeed in the industry.

As mentioned earlier, film school is a breeding ground for making contacts in the industry. Often, contacts are the essential factor in getting a job; many Hollywood insiders agree that it's not what you know but who you know that will get you in. Networking often leads to good opportunities at various types of jobs in the industry. Many professionals recommend that those who want to become directors should go to Los Angeles or New York, find any industry-related job, continue to take classes, and keep their eyes and ears open for news of job openings, especially with those professionals who are admired for their talent.

A program to be aware of is the Assistant Directors Training Program of the Directors Guild of America (their address is listed at the end of this article). This program provides an excellent opportunity to those without industry connections to work on film and television productions. Trainees are placed with major studios or on television movies and series. They work for 400 days and earn between $521 and $640 per week, with the salary increasing every 100 days. Once they have completed the program, they become freelance second assistant directors and can join the guild. The competition is extremely stiff for these positions; the program accepts only 16 to 20 trainees from among some 800 to 1,200 applicants each year.

Keep in mind that Hollywood is not everything. Directors work on documentaries, on television productions, and with various types of video presentations, from music to business. Honing skills at these types of jobs is beneficial for those still intent on directing the big screen.

Advancement

In the motion picture industry, advancement often comes with recognition. Directors who work on well-received movies are given awards as well as further job offers. Probably the most glamorized trophy is the Academy Award: the Oscar. Oscars are awarded in 24 categories, including one for best achievement in directing, and are given annually at a gala to recognize the outstanding accomplishments of those in the field.

Candidates for Oscars are usually judged by peers. Directors who have not worked on films popular enough to have made it in Hollywood should nevertheless seek recognition from reputable organizations. One such group is the National Endowment for the Arts, an independent agency of the U.S. government that supports and awards artists, including those who work in film. The endowment provides financial assistance in the form of fellowships and grants to those seen as contributing to the excellence of arts in the country.

Earnings

Directors' salaries vary greatly. Most Hollywood film directors are members of the Directors Guild of America, and salaries (as well as hours of work and other employment conditions) are usually negotiated by this union. Generally, contracts provide for minimum weekly salaries and follow a basic trend depending on the cost of the picture being produced: for film budgets over $1.5 million, the weekly salary is about $8,000; for budgets of $500,000 to $1.5 million, it is $5,800 per week; and for budgets under $500,000, the weekly salary is $5,100. Motion picture art directors earn an average weekly salary of about $1,850; directors of photography, $2,000. Keep in mind that because directors are freelancers, they may have no income for many weeks out of the year.

Although contracts usually provide only for the minimum rate of pay, most directors earn more, and they often negotiate extra conditions. Woody Allen, for example, takes the minimum salary required by the union for directing a film but also receives at least 10 percent of the film's gross receipts.

Salaries for directors who work in television vary greatly based on type of project and employer and on whether the director is employed as a freelancer or as a salaried employee. A director at a small-market station may average as little as $28,000 per year, while a director employed by a larger network affiliate may make up to $120,000 annually.

The U.S. Department of Labor reports that the median annual salary of film directors was $50,280 in 2000. Television directors earned approximately $34,630 a year. Among all directors, the lowest 10 percent earned less than $21,050, and the highest 10 percent earned more than $87,770.

Work Environment

The work of the director is considered glamorous and prestigious, and of course directors have been known to become quite famous. But directors work under great stress, meeting deadlines, staying within budgets, and resolving problems among staff. "Nine-to-five" definitely does not describe a day in the life of a director; 16-hour days (and more) are not uncommon. Because directors are ultimately responsible for so much, schedules often dictate that they become immersed in their work around the clock, from pre-production to final cut. Nonetheless, those able to make it in the industry find their work to be extremely enjoyable and satisfying.

Outlook

According to the U.S. Department of Labor, employment for motion picture and television directors is expected to grow faster than the average for all occupations through 2010. This optimistic forecast is based on the increasing global demand for films and television programming made in the United States as well as continuing U.S. demand for home video and DVD rentals. However, competition is extreme and turnover is high. Most positions in the motion picture industry are held on a freelance basis. As is the case with most film industry workers, directors are usually hired to work on one film at a time. After a film is completed, new contacts must be made for further assignments.

Television offers directors a wider variety of employment opportunities such as directing sitcoms, made-for-television movies, newscasts, commercials, even music videos. Cable television networks are proliferating, and directors are needed to help create original programming to fill this void. Half of all television directors work as freelancers. This number is predicted to rise as more cable networks and production companies attempt to cut costs by hiring directors on a project-to-project basis.

For More Information

For information about colleges with film and television programs of study, contact:

American Film Institute
2021 North Western Avenue
Los Angeles, CA 90027
Tel: 323-856-7600
Email: info@afionline.org
Web: http://www.afionline.org

For information on scholarships and grants and to receive free monthly email newsletters, contact:

Broadcast Education Association
1771 N Street, NW
Washington, DC 20036-2891
Tel: 888-380-7222
Email: beainfo@beaweb.org
Web: http://www.beaweb.org

For information about the Assistant Directors Training Program and other resources, contact:

Directors Guild of America
7920 Sunset Boulevard
Los Angeles, California 90046
Tel: 310-289-2000
Email: trainingprogram@dgptp.org
Web: http://www.dga.org

Film and Television Extras

School Subjects	Speech Theater/dance
Personal Skills	Artistic Following instructions
Work Environment	Indoors and outdoors Primarily multiple locations
Minimum Education Level	High school diploma
Salary Range	$500 to $5,000 to $15,000
Certification or Licensing	None available
Outlook	Faster than the average

Overview

Film and television extras, also known as *background performers,* have the non-speaking roles in films and TV shows. They work in the background of film scenes, following the orders of directors and crew members. They may work in crowd scenes, or may simply be one of a few people among the principal performers.

History

Ever since the dawn of filmmaking over 100 years ago, filmmakers have understood the importance of using extras to lend authenticity to a scene. Particularly in the silent era, visual effects were very important; people were employed to move about the makeshift sets of a film production to help viewers understand the size of the city portrayed, the number of people affected by the film's events, and other details. D. W. Griffith's *Intolerance,* made in 1916, is one of the earliest and most infamous examples of a big-budget production that relied a great deal on extravagant sets and huge crowd scenes. Extras were dressed in a variety of period costume and recreated epic battle scenes. In one sequence, extras storm the immense walls of ancient Babylon; in another, extras play factory workers shot down by police. Today, large crowd scenes are still used in big productions to provide scenes with greater power and scope. Though computer-generated images were used to fill out the crowd scenes of such films as *Elizabeth* and *Titanic,* many extras were still used. For *Titanic,* these extras were filmed in costume in a room, then later added to the deck of the digitally created ship.

The Job

When you go to the movies, you probably don't pay too close attention to the people in the background of all the scenes. Yet, if they weren't there—if there were no lines at the bank, no crowds at the football game, no passengers on the airplane—you'd certainly notice. Practically every filmmaker uses extras. Though these extras don't have lines, close-ups, or any real significance to the film's plot, they are important in establishing the world of the film.

Many people work as extras to gain professional experience, hoping to someday become *principal actors* (performers in featured roles), or to work in the film industry in some other capacity. Others, like John Sharpe, simply see extra work as an enjoyable way to supplement their incomes. "I work mostly with shows and movies that need high school and college-age looking kids," Sharpe says. Recently, he spent nine days on the set of the film *She's All That.* His TV credits include *Buffy the Vampire Slayer* and *Party of Five.*

"It's easy to become an extra," he says. "Anyone can register at a nonunion extra casting agency. There are several of them in the Los Angeles area. When you have a day you can work, you call their recorded line and see if they need anyone of your description. If so, you call an agent in their office and they book you for it."

If selected, film and TV extras are advised on what they need to bring to the set, and when and where to report to work. For most films, extras are asked to wear their own clothes. For a film set in another time period, they may have to report to the wardrobe department for a costume fitting.

In some cases, a casting director for a film will be looking for specific types and talents. For example, if a scene features a baseball game, the director may need extras who can pitch, hit, and run. Or a period scene in a dance hall may call for extras who know certain traditional dances. These extras are called *special ability extras* and usually receive better daily pay than general extras. A *stand-in* may also be needed for a film shoot. A stand-in is an extra who takes the place of a principal actor when the crew prepares to film a scene, but who is not actually filmed. Stand-ins are positioned on the set for the cameras to focus the shot and set up lights.

Members of the Screen Actors Guild (SAG), the union for film actors and extras, generally receive better pay than nonunion extras. A film must have 30 SAG-registered extras on a given day before hiring nonunion extras.

When reporting for work, extras may be part of a rehearsal or may be thrust immediately into the filming of the scene. They are required to pay close attention to the director and cooperate with crew members. Extras may be asked to simply stand in the background, to have conversation with other extras, or to move freely about the set. They must keep track of what they are doing in each scene in order to help maintain continuity from scene to scene. Extras may have to repeat their actions, gestures, and expressions again and again until the filmmakers have the shot they need. Their scene may only take a few hours to complete or may take several days. Extras may be used for the background in only one scene or may be used in many scenes. In rare cases, an extra is plucked from a crowd scene and given a line to speak. In this case, the performer is considered a *day player*.

Requirements

High School

Many children and high school students work as extras in TV shows and films. Though you won't need special training to become a film extra, you should at least obtain a high school diploma. Classes that may be helpful to you in your work as an extra include theater, dance, and speech.

Other Requirements

Union membership can be helpful in finding work and earning better pay, but it isn't required for you to work as an extra. Generally, performers apply for SAG membership after finding success in working as an extra for a time. See the end of the article for SAG's contact information to learn more.

Extras need to be punctual, attentive, and capable of following instructions closely. "You need to be responsible and dependable first and foremost," John Sharpe says.

Extras should also be patient, as they may spend much of their time waiting around, or doing the same things repeatedly.

Employers

Because of the nature of the work, extras don't have a regular employer, though they may work for some of the same filmmakers and TV productions. In addition to movies and TV shows, extras are needed for commercials, music videos, and interactive games.

Starting Out

For regular work as a film or TV extra, you'll have more success living where the bulk of films and TV shows are filmed, around Los Angeles or New York. Though some productions may place ads for extras in local newspapers or on the Internet, you will benefit the most by having an agent. There are agents who work exclusively with extras, as opposed to principal actors agents. Extras agents typically charge a registration fee (usually under $30) and a 5 to 10 percent commission. When selecting an agent, be very careful of scams; carefully read any contract and be wary of agents with large registration fees or those who "guarantee" work. For information about reputable agents, you can check with your local film commission or local division of SAG.

Advancement

Becoming a member of SAG ensures extras and other performers better pay. Union membership can also help to establish contacts and possibly locate more work. "If you plan to pursue acting, extra work is probably the best way into SAG," Sharpe says. "Spending so much time on sets is a good way to learn about the industry and even to make connections."

By talking to other extras and crew members, beginning performers can learn more about the film industry and may make some valuable connections. Unfortunately, there are no guarantees for success in the film industry; even years of experience in the industry may eventually lead nowhere. However, extras may be able to use connections they've made through union membership and working on productions to get more major auditions for supporting or major roles on films and TV shows.

Earnings

It is very rare that someone is able to make a living solely from work as an extra. According to SAG, a majority of its 90,000 members make less than $7,5000 a year. SAG sets daily wage minimums for its members, which vary according to city and type of extra work. For example, in 2002, extras working on the West Coast made at least $110 a day. If they had a part showing off a special ability or talent, they were paid $120 or more a day. Extras also earn more if they have to work in rain or smoke, or if they are required to wear body makeup, wigs, or a certain haircut for the part. If they supply their own props, such as pets, cars, golf clubs, or luggage, extras also are paid higher daily rates.

Any extra who is upgraded to a speaking part—even just one line of dialogue—is considered a day player and earns significantly more per day.

Work Environment

The work of a film or TV extra is unsteady, but many people enjoy the opportunity to see themselves on screen. Though the work isn't terribly glamorous, extas do have the chance to see famous actors and filmmakers practice their craft. Extras can work indoors on a set or outdoors at a remote location. They work under heavy lights and may be required to do the same things over and over. There may also be a great deal of downtime as extras wait for cast and crew to prepare for a shot. "It's not rare to work a 12- to 14-hour day," John Sharpe says, "so you need to be flexible."

Outlook

According to the American Theater Association, more than 350,000 adults act every year. Because of the fierce competition, jobs in the film industry are hard to come by. Extras who live in Los Angeles or New York City and have an extras agent are more likely be able to find work, but the low pay and the unsteady nature of the work usually prevent them from making a comfortable living as an extra.

The U.S. Department of Labor predicts employment in the film and TV industry to grow faster than the average through 2010. Though the competition for jobs is high, many individuals leave acting for a more stable and higher income. Because of the high turnover, opportunities for work are always available; performers with patience, confidence, and stamina will stand a higher chance at success in the acting business.

For More Information

For information about membership, wages, and advice on filmmaking and acting, contact the following unions:

International Alliance of Theatrical Stage Employees, Moving Picture Technicians, Artists and Allied Crafts of the United States and Canada (IATSE)
1430 Broadway, 20th Floor
New York, NY 10018
Tel: 212-730-1770
Web: http://www.iatse.lm.com

Screen Actors Guild (SAG)
5757 Wilshire Boulevard
Los Angeles, CA 90036-3600
Tel: 323-954-1600
Web: http://www.sag.com

Magicians

Speech Theater/dance	School Subjects
Artistic Mechanical/manipulative	Personal Skills
Primarily indoors Primarily multiple locations	Work Environment
High school diploma	Minimum Education Level
$50 (for a single show) to $20,000 to $120,000+	Salary Range
None available	Certification or Licensing
About as fast as the average	Outlook

Overview

Magicians perform illusions to mystify and entertain audiences. They use quick hand movements and a variety of other techniques to perform classic tricks such as pulling a rabbit out of a hat or making a handkerchief disappear. They often use props, such as illusion boxes, scarves, cards, and coins. Magicians may perform in front of small audiences or entertain thousands of people in large theaters or on television. They generally work alone, but may have one or two assistants help with more involved performances. Because most magicians work independently, it is difficult to determine how many are working; the International Brotherhood of Magicians reports approximately 15,000 members.

History

Magic has its origins in ancient Mesopotamia and Egypt. The biblical account of Moses and Aaron in the Pharaoh's Court recounts how the Pharaoh's wise men and sorcerers cast down their rods and the rods became serpents. According to some explanations, this feat was performed with serpents that were hypnotized so as to be stiff and lifeless. When the serpents were thrown down, they awoke and crawled away.

The earliest practitioners of magic were religious priests, who used the illusion of supernatural events to maintain control over the population at large. In fact, the word "magician" derives from the word "magus," an ancient Persian priest. Priests would perform elaborate rituals that included illusions such as burning doors and talking spirits to persuade people to do or believe certain things. Magical spells were also used to scare off evil spirits or to induce rain or other natural events.

Because magic conjured up images of the supernatural, practitioners of magic were long viewed with a combination of respect and fear. Often, people were mistrustful of magicians or those associated with the supernatural and came to view them as sorcerers. During the 1300s in Europe, magic was called a form of witchcraft and considered heresy. Those who practiced magic, or were simply accused of practicing magic, were shunned and in some cases killed. During the 1700s and 1800s in North America, several people regarded as witches or sorcerers were burned at the stake.

In recent times, magic has lost some of its mystery and has become acknowledged and accepted as a performance art. Influential performers, such as the Sicilian Count Alessandro di Cagliostro (1743-95), the Frenchman Robert-Houdin (1805-71), and the American Harry Houdini (1874-1926) have captured the imaginations of audiences through a combination of skill, training, and imagination. Today, well-known magicians such as David Copperfield entertain people all over the world. More controversial are the popular and less traditional duo Penn & Teller, who sometimes reveal the secrets of their illusions.

The Job

Magicians should be good actors, able to create and maintain an atmosphere of excitement and intrigue. They are masters of illusion. Magicians do one thing, while an audience sees another. Through a combination of "hocus-pocus" and persuasive comments, a magician can appear to pull flowers from a magic wand, levitate a person in the air, and perform a wide variety of other tricks.

There are two basic elements to a magician's performance. The first element is the technique, which is the actual mechanics of performing a set of illusions or tricks. A magician must practice each movement of any trick over and over until the illusion can be executed perfectly. For example, in a trick often called "After the Flood," a magician pours water into a large, rectangular box and then removes various animals (birds, ducks, squirrels, etc.) from the box. To top it off, the magician reveals a reclining person in the rectangular box, and no water in sight. This illusion seems impossible; not only is the box rather small to accommodate this assortment of animals and human subjects, and leaves the audience wondering what happened to the water.

The reality behind the illusion reveals a mechanical engineering masterpiece. This is where technique becomes crucial to the success of the trick. The magician must rehearse it repeatedly to ensure the greatest illusion without revealing any of his or her technique. Any error in the presentation, and audience members might be tipped off as to how the illusion is done. As a result, magicians jealously guard the secrets behind their illusions. Many hours are spent practicing illusions that might be performed in just several minutes.

The second key element to success in magic is presentation. Magicians must know not only how to do a trick, but how to be entertaining. If the illusions are not presented in an exciting fashion, many audiences will lose interest.

A successful magic show may combine elements of storytelling and comedy with drama and suspense. Magicians should be able to shift from one illusion to another in a logical and smooth fashion. The individual tricks should be arranged and sequenced so as to constitute a complete performance that has variety and a theme. This emphasis on the presentation of a show means that many magicians spend as much time on perfecting the delivery of an illusion as they do on practicing the techniques of the illusion itself.

It has been said that the best magicians are actors who play the part of magicians. This means they can tell a story and get the audience so enthralled with the performance that the audience sometimes forgets they are watching an actual magic show. Like other actors, magicians must have a sense of timing and a stage presence.

Magicians are constantly interacting with their audiences. Often, magicians will ask for volunteers from audiences as part of their routines. A magician might ask an audience member to pick a card from a group of cards, for example, and then have that same card reappear some other place in the auditorium. Or a magician may invite a volunteer to stand up on stage to discover that his or her wallet has disappeared without detection. Of course, the good—and ethical—magician will give it back!

An important ingredient of working effectively with audience members is to remember that a magician always works to entertain people without making them feel silly or embarrassed. Magicians should never create comic situations by ridiculing an audience member.

Magicians work with many different types of materials. A single performance can include cards, illusion boxes, magnets, chairs, balls, scarves, swords, and other props. A magician might also perform hypnosis on audience participants or escape from handcuffs, ropes, or chains.

Some magicians combine magic tricks with acrobatic stunts, such as flying through the air while holding an audience member. Shows can be quite spectacular: one magician has even made the Statue of Liberty seemingly disappear!

Although many magicians perform similar tricks, each magician brings his or her unique style to the performance. Individual magicians will establish a certain set of illusions to put together a show. Of course, these shows will vary somewhat, but generally magicians will have a set routine that they perform over and over. The most successful magicians, however, constantly work to present their illusions in new ways and to add new and more exciting illusions to their shows.

It takes a high degree of skill to perform illusions. The more skilled and experienced the magician, the more intricate the magic. Some tricks can be relatively simple, such as pulling a certain card out of a deck of cards, but most tricks require great skill and can even be somewhat dangerous. Sword swallowing, for example, takes much practice (and courage!) to stretch the throat muscles.

Magicians generally set up their shows several hours before performances. They may lay mats, set up tables and chairs, or place objects into concealed containers. Often, assistants will do this preparation work, while the magician supervises to ensure that all props are properly placed. More elaborate performances may require the efforts of a team to set up and execute illusions.

Assistants are often involved in the many tricks and stunts performed, such as appearing out of hiding as part of an illusion. They may also help distract the audience's attention while the magician performs the trick. Assistants also help magicians clean up after a performance.

Sometimes two or more magicians will perform at the same time, combining their skills and ideas in a show. The magicians might perform tricks together or they might perform separately, showing the audience a greater variety of illusions. A magician might also perform with a clown, comedian, or other entertainer.

Requirements

High School

There are no formal educational requirements for becoming a magician. People generally do not take college or high school courses to learn magic, although courses in acting or public speaking can help a magician become more effective. Some magic clubs or magic stores may offer basic classes on performance techniques.

Postsecondary Training

Because most magicians work part-time, they may have college degrees in unrelated fields, such as business, law, or political science. Other magicians have degrees in more related fields, such as drama or speech communications.

Although there are few formal training options, magicians usually work independently at becoming proficient at their craft. They are skilled entertainers. It can take years of practice and training to become an accomplished magician, yet it is often possible to learn some of the more basic tricks in just a short time. They should be able to learn tricks from a variety of sources (primarily other magicians, videotapes, or books on magic) and refine their techniques through practice.

Magicians should have at least a basic understanding of mathematics and good business skills in order to handle their own financial affairs.

Other Requirements

A magician should have a strong imagination, not only to visualize tricks that may not have been tried before, but also to be able to perform standard tricks in a somewhat new and creative fashion. Many tricks or stunts have been performed for over 100 years, yet with a unique flair, these tricks can be performed in a fresh manner.

It is important for a magician to be comfortable performing before various groups of people. They may perform at a children's birthday party one day, for example, and the next day perform before a group of adults in a nightclub. For magicians who perform frequently, it is important to be able to do the same tricks over and over while retaining a fresh approach to the performance.

In a magic show, the actual illusion might not be as important as how it is executed. For this reason, it is vital that a magician has a strong stage presence and effective speaking style. Creating an atmosphere requires the ability to tell a story, interweaving tricks throughout the performance. Many magicians use music, colored lights, curtains, and other enhancements to create a festive or mysterious mood.

Magicians need good hand-eye coordination to perform tricks smoothly. They also should be agile to quickly move wooden boxes, tables, or other props. Many magicians build their own equipment; as a result, woodworking and other related skills are useful.

Exploring

Aspiring magicians can find many opportunities for practice, especially given the fact that many everyday household items can be used in tricks, such as ropes, balls, and coins. There are many books and videotapes, as well as beginner magic kits, available that explain how to do the basic tricks. With a little practice and not much expense, anyone can put on a short magic show. In addition, some high schools or other organizations sponsor magic clubs, where those interested in magic can meet to discuss techniques.

Once you have developed and practiced a routine, perform for friends and family. Magic clubs may also give you opportunities to perform. Any chance to practice tricks in front of an audience will help to develop your skills and confidence as a magician.

Perhaps the best way to learn about becoming a magician is to work as a magician's assistant. In this position, you can observe how illusions are performed and also get a feel for the day-to-day demands of performing.

Employers

Magicians generally are freelance performers, hired for everything from private parties to major stage shows on Broadway or in Las Vegas. Although a large number of magicians perform at magic clubs, many also perform for school and church groups.

Some businesses hire magicians to perform at trade shows and sales meetings to improve interest in a product. Magicians generally perform their standard routines at these shows, though they may incorporate the client's product into the act. Some magicians choose not to get involved in these marketing-style magic shows, because they may not wish to use their craft to promote a particular product.

Starting Out

Many people become magicians after serving as assistants to more accomplished magicians. These apprenticeships are generally informal in nature and vary in duration from several months to several years. It is also possible for someone to begin practicing as a magician while still working as an assistant.

One reason many magicians start as apprentices is that professional magicians rarely reveal in public how they perform their tricks. (Otherwise everyone would soon know how a trick is done, and there would be no element of surprise.) Assistants get a behind-the-scenes look at how tricks are done and in this way learn impressive illusions.

Some magicians may start on their own without serving as assistants. These magicians learn techniques from friends, classes, or books and videotapes and then develop their own routines. When novice magicians feel qualified to perform a show, they may advertise. The first performances may be relatively short and simple, such as a child's birthday party, for example. As they develop skills and a good reputation, the performances will expand in difficulty, complexity, and duration.

Advancement

Most magicians perform on a part-time basis, either in the evenings or on weekends. There are very few who can make this a full-time profession. Many magicians perform for free or for very little money, finding satisfaction in simply performing. For those with a great deal of skill and initiative, it is possible to develop a reputation and find work in several communities. In rare cases, magicians develop national reputations and perform in large clubs and on television, such as David Copperfield.

Individuals who have a mind for both magic and business may choose to buy a magic club or a magic shop. This requires a great deal of money and risk, so the magician should be financially stable before investing.

Earnings

While world famous magicians such as Harry Blackstone, Lance Burton, Siegfried and Roy, and David Copperfield can earn many thousands of dollars for each performance, most magicians do not earn enough from their performances to support themselves financially. The vast majority of magicians perform on nights or weekends while still holding full- or part-time jobs. What they earn as magicians varies depending on their reputation and audience, from $50 for performing at a birthday party to several thousand dollars for performing at a business meeting or large magic show. According to the Society of American Magicians, those who work as magicians as a side career may earn as much as $15,000 to $20,000 per year, while full-time professionals may earn as much as $60,000 to $120,000 per year.

Most magicians perform more as a hobby than a profession. These individuals perform magic for the sheer love and excitement of the craft.

Working as independent professionals, magicians generally have to provide for their own health insurance and retirement fund. However, some professional organizations, such as the Society of American Magicians, provide group insurance rates.

Work Environment

Magicians generally perform indoors in magic clubs, small theaters, homes, and schools. They arrive at a performance site several hours early to set up props and place any hidden objects.

Although performances may run less than an hour, magicians spend many more hours practicing their routines so that everything goes exactly as planned. They have to be able to perform under pressure, maintaining their composure and timing in front of an attentive audience.

Most magicians work on a part-time basis, performing at night or on weekends. They may have to do quite a bit of traveling to get from show to show. Some may find it challenging to perform the same routines over and over while still making each show fresh and original. Others spend a great deal of time creating new illusions and perfecting new routines.

Magicians should be able to work closely with their assistants. It is vital to create an atmosphere of trust as teamwork is often needed to perform intricate illusions.

Despite the long hours required to polish their routines, magicians should enjoy entertaining. Their hard work is paid off when they amaze and astonish audiences through their array of illusions.

Outlook

Magic is a performance art, and like other performance artists, magicians face an uncertain employment picture. If the economy is strong, there will be a greater demand for magicians because people will have more disposable income to spend on entertainment. If the economy is weaker, magicians will have greater difficulty finding work. In short, there will continue to be employment, though these opportunities will often be for part-time assignments. Because magicians must compete with a growing number of entertainment options, growth in this field is likely to remain about as fast as the average. Jobs in the business arena should continue through the next decade and create some well-paying opportunities for those with the skills and versatility to entertain business people.

As in other fields, those with the most skills and experience should find better job opportunities, while those just beginning may find it more difficult to secure employment. However, with hard work and a love for magic, magicians of all ages and skill levels should find opportunities to perform.

For More Information

For information on conventions, publications, and local groups (called RINGS) that provide lectures and demonstrations, contact:

International Brotherhood of Magicians
11155 South Towne Square, Suite C
St. Louis, MO 63123-7813
Tel: 314-845-9200
Email: office@magician.org
Web: http://www.magician.org

For information on local organizations, publications, programs for younger members, and the insurance program, contact:

Society of American Magicians
PO Box 510260
St. Louis, MO 63151
Tel: 314-846-5659
Web: http://www.magicsam.com

Music Conductors and Directors

Music Theater/dance	School Subjects
Artistic Communication/ideas	Personal Skills
Primarily indoors Primarily one location	Work Environment
High school diploma	Minimum Education Level
$15,000 to $40,000 to $500,000+	Salary Range
None available	Certification or Licensing
About as fast as the average	Outlook

Overview

Music conductors direct large groups of musicians or singers in the performance of a piece of music. There are various types of conductors, including those who lead symphony orchestras, dance bands, marching bands, and choral groups. They use their hands, a baton, or both to indicate the musical sound variations and timing of a composition. Their chief concern is their interpretation of how a piece of music should be played. They are responsible for rehearsing the orchestra and auditioning musicians for positions in the ensemble.

Conductors must have the complete respect of the musicians they lead. The great conductors have a personal charisma that awes both musician and listener alike. Conductors are unique in the modern musical world in that they make no sound themselves yet control the sound that others make. The orchestra is their instrument. Music conductors sometimes carry the title of *music director,* which implies a wider area of responsibilities, including administrative and managerial duties.

History

The origins of music conducting remain quite obscure. Some form of time-keeping undoubtedly went on even among primitive musical groups. In early orchestral days, timekeeping was often done orally, with the use of a scroll, or by pounding a long stick on the floor. During the 18th century, a musician often kept time, usually the organist or harpsichordist or the chief of the first violinists, who came to be called "concertmaster" in modern times. There were no specialist conductors at this time; the composer generally served as the conductor, and he usually conducted only his own works. The concertmaster role grew increasingly more important, and for a period it was not unusual for him to keep time by stamping his feet even when there was a separate conductor who might also keep time by clapping his hands or tapping a desk. Needless to say, this simultaneous stamping and clapping could be very irritating to musicians and audience alike.

Just when the baton was first used is not known, but mention of using a staff in this manner was made in Greek mythology as early as 709 BC. It is known that batons were used since the eighth century and became fashionable, as orchestras grew larger, in the late 18th century. By the mid-19th century their usage was a widely accepted practice.

Early in the history of the orchestra, most concert music was performed in conjunction with opera. In 1816, noted French violinist Rodolphe Kreutzer used his violin bow to conduct the Paris Opera. In 1824, the Opera employed the services of a specialist conductor, the noted violinist Françoise Antoine Habeneck, who also conducted with a bow, and who, in 1828 became one of the first to establish an orchestra devoted entirely to concert as opposed to opera music. The first Beethoven symphonies heard in Paris were conducted by Habeneck. During these early days of conducting, it was common for the conductor to face the audience rather than the orchestra, a practice that was still common in Russia during the late 19th century.

In 1776, *Kapellmeister* Johann Reichardt conducted the Berlin Court Opera with a baton, possibly the first to do so. Early in the 19th century, Ludwig Spohr (1784-1859) was perhaps the first musician to be recognized purely as a conductor and was another of the early users of the baton rather than the bow or a paper scroll. The baton was at first a rather large and awkward device similar to the instrument used by a drum major. Hector Berlioz (1803-69) used such a baton in his white-gloved hand. Felix Mendelssohn (1808-47) used a scroll or a stick; he was particularly notable for the grandeur of his style. Mendelssohn also regularly cut and reorchestrated the compositions he conducted, a practice that has continued. Some conductors of the period eschewed the baton and used their bare hands. This practice was never widely adopted, although a few great conductors, including Leopold Stokowski (1882-1977), preferred the bare hand method.

Another innovation was the use of the full score by conductors. Before the full score was available, conductors usually read from the first violinist's part. Berlioz was one of the first to employ the full score and was one of the great 19th century composer-conductors who influenced conducting style into the next century. Among the other major influences were Felix Mendelssohn and Richard Wagner (1813-83). These men assumed full, autocratic command of the orchestra, each insisting on strict obedience from the musicians in carrying out the conductor's interpretation of the music. Each developed his own characteristic style, which brought him widespread adulation. Berlioz had an inspirational effect on the orchestra and, while his physical style was flamboyant, he was rather inflexible in his tempo. Mendelssohn was also strict in his timing, while Wagner took a more flexible approach.

Among the conductors influenced by Wagner were such notable figures as Hans von Bulow, Franz Liszt (1811-86), and Wilhelm Furtwangler (1886-1954). Mendelssohn's followers included Karl Muck, Felix Weingartner (1863-1942), and Richard Strauss (1864-1949), all distinctive for their minimal baton movement and methodical tempos. Some conductors defied categorization, however. One of these was Gustav Mahler (1860-1911) in the late 19th century; he wielded a tyrannical power over the orchestra and flew into rages that became legendary.

Many different conducting styles emerged in the 20th century, including some that were highly exhibitionistic. One of the extremes of that type was exemplified by Sir Thomas Beecham (1879-1961), the great British conductor. He sometimes raised his arms skyward imploring the orchestra to reach perfection; at other times he lunged at the horn section to raise its power, occasionally falling off the podium in his exuberance. Leopold Stokowski and Leonard Bernstein (1918-90) have also been noted for their dramatic exhibitionism. In the early 1920s in Russia, an attempt was made at forming a conductorless orchestra, undoubtedly an attempt at eliminating the dictatorial rule of the conductor. The experiment died out after a few years, although in the late 1920s conductorless experiments were attempted in New York City and Budapest.

The number of outstanding conductors in the 20th century are too numerous to mention, but one name is perhaps legendary above all others. This would be Arturo Toscanini (1867-1957), originally an opera composer, whose infallible ear, musicianship, comprehensive knowledge of scores, and orchestral control made him virtually the prototype of great 20th century conductors. At rehearsals his famed temper flared as he exhorted his charges to perfectly perform his interpretation of a score. Before the audience he exuded charisma. Toscanini, who conducted the New York Philharmonic-

Symphony from 1928 to 1936 and the NBC Symphony from 1937 to 1954, was perhaps the most influential conductor of the mid-20th century, his main rival being Furtwangler in Germany. Some conductors of the late 20th century, however, remained free of both influences. Perhaps the most notable of these is Sir Georg Solti (1912-1997), who, with large and seemingly awkward movements, inspired his musicians to brilliant heights of musical perfection. Many authorities acknowledge that under his guidance the Chicago Symphony Orchestra became one of the finest musical ensembles of the late 20th century. While many women have taken their places among the great orchestras of the world, few have been able to move into the field of conducting. In the second half of the 20th century, however, there were some breakthroughs, and a number of women conductors, such as Sarah Caldwell in the United States, achieved notable recognition.

The Job

Conducting, whether it be of a symphony orchestra, an opera, a chorus, a theater pit orchestra, a marching band, or even a "big" swing band, is an enormously complex and demanding occupation to which only the exceptional individual can possibly aspire with hope of even moderate success. Music conductors must have multiple skills and talents. First and foremost, they must be consummate musicians. Not only should they have mastered an instrument, but they also must know music and be able to interpret the score of any composition. They should have an unerring ear and a bearing that commands the respect of the musicians. Conductors need to be sensitive to the musicians, sympathetic to their problems, and able to inspire them to bring out the very best they have to offer. Conductors must also have a sense of showmanship. Some conductors have advanced farther than others because their dramatic conducting style helps bring in larger audiences and greater receipts. The conductor must also be a psychologist who can deal with the multiplicity of complex and temperamental personalities presented by a large ensemble of musicians and singers. Composers must exude personal charm; orchestras are always fund-raising, and the composer is frequently expected to meet major donors to keep their good will. Finally, and in line with fundraising, music conductors and directors are expected to have administrative skills and to understand the business and financial problems that face the orchestra organization.

Conductors are distinguished by their baton technique and arm and body movements. These can vary widely from conductor to conductor, some being reserved and holding to minimal movements, others using sweeping baton strokes and broad arm and body gestures. There is no right or wrong way to conduct; it is a highly individualized art, and great conductors produce excellent results using extremely contrasting styles. The conductor's fundamental purpose in leading, regardless of style, is to set the tempo and rhythm of a piece. Conductors must be sure that the orchestra is following their interpretation of the music, and they must resolve any problems that the score poses. Failure to render a composition in a way that is pleasing to the public and the critics is usually blamed on the conductor, although there is a school that feels that both the conductor and the musicians are to blame, or that at least it is difficult to tell which one is most at fault.

The quality of a performance is probably most directly related to the conductor's rehearsal techniques. It is during rehearsals that conductors must diagnose and correct to their satisfaction the musical, interpretive, rhythmic, balance, and intonation problems encountered by the orchestra. They must work with each unit of the orchestra individually and the entire ensemble as a whole; this may include soloist instrumentalists and singers as well as a chorus. Some conductors rehearse every detail of a score while others have been known to emphasize only certain parts during rehearsal. Some are quiet and restrained at rehearsals, while others work to a feverish emotional pitch. The sound that an orchestra makes is also identified with the conductor, and for some, such as Eugene Ormandy (1899-1985), formerly of the Philadelphia Orchestra, the tone of an orchestra becomes a recognizable signature. Tone is determined by the conductor's use of the various sections of the orchestra. The brass section, for instance, can be instructed to play so that the sound is bright, sharp, and piercing, or they can play to produce a rich, sonorous, and heavy sound. The strings can play the vibrato broadly to produce a thick, lush tone or play with little vibrato to produce a thinner, more delicate sound.

Requirements

High School

Formal training in at least one musical instrument is necessary for a future as a music conductor or director. Keyboard instruction is particularly important. In high school, participation in a concert band, jazz ensemble, choir, or orchestra will teach you about group performing and how the various parts contribute to a whole sound. Some high schools may offer opportunities to conduct school music groups.

Postsecondary Training

It is unlikely that many people start out at a very early point in life to become a music conductor. Most conductors begin studying music at an early age and possibly, at some later, more mature point of life may discover or suspect that they have the qualities to become a conductor. Some conductors become involved at the high school or college level leading a small group for whom they may also do the arranging and possibly some composing. There are some courses specifically in conducting at advanced institutions, and interested students may take courses in composition, arranging, and orchestrating, which provide a good background for conducting. Some opportunities to conduct may arise in the university, and you may be able to study with a faculty member who conducts the school orchestra. There are also conductor training programs and apprenticeship programs, which are announced in the music trade papers.

It was once commonly thought that conducting was unteachable. That attitude has been changing, however, and some institutions have developed formalized programs to teach the art of conducting. The Paris Conservatory is particularly noted for its conducting instruction, and completion of that institution's course is said to pave the way to opportunities in conducting. The Julliard School is another institution known for its studies in conducting.

Conductors must acquire a multiplicity of skills in order to practice their art. These skills may be divided into three parts: technical, performance, and conducting.

Technical skills deal with conductors' ability to control orchestral intonation, balance, and color; they must be advanced at sight reading and transposition in order to cope with orchestral scores. Conductors must acquire a comprehensive knowledge of all orchestral instruments and must themselves have mastery of at least one instrument, the piano probably being the most helpful. They must acquire skills in composition and music analysis, which presumes accomplished skills in counterpoint, harmony, musical structures, and orchestration. Finally, conductors must understand and be able to adapt musical styling.

Performance skills refer to conductors' own instrumental ability. Mastery of one instrument is important, but the more instruments conductors know, the better they will be able to relate to members of the orchestra. It is through knowledge of instruments that conductors develop their interpretive abilities.

Conducting skills involve the ability to use the baton and to control the timing, rhythm, and structure of a musical piece. Conductors must develop these skills at performances and at rehearsals. At rehearsals they must use their power and their intellect to blend the various elements of the orchestra and the composition into a single unified presentation. Conductors must also learn to use their whole bodies, along with the baton, to control the music.

Conductors require not only an extensive knowledge of music but also a strong general background in the arts and humanities. They should have a comprehensive knowledge of musical history as it fits into the general fabric of civilization along with competence in various languages, including French, German, Italian, and Latin. Language skills are particularly helpful in coaching singers. Familiarity with the history of Western civilization, particularly its literature, drama, and art, will also be valuable in the composer's musical frame of reference.

Other Requirements

Conductors require a high degree of self-discipline and unquestioned integrity in order to fill a difficult and complex leadership role. It is important as well that they learn all the aspects of the business and social functions of an orchestra.

Like musicians and composers, conductors must have talent, a quality that cannot be taught or acquired. They must have supreme self-confidence in their ability to lead and interpret the music of the great masters. They must convince both audience and ensemble that they are in command.

Exploring

The best way to become familiar with the art of conducting is to study music and the great conductors themselves. It is not possible to understand conducting beyond the most superficial level without a good background in music. Students of conducting should go to as many musical presentations as they can, such as symphonies, operas, and musical theater, and study the conductors, noting their baton techniques and their arm and body movements. Try to determine how the orchestra and audience respond to the gesturing of the conductors. There are also many associations, reference books, and biographies that provide detailed information about conductors and their art. One of the most prominent organizations is the American

Symphony Orchestra League located in Washington, DC. It holds a national conference and conducting workshops each year.

Employers

There are many situations in which music conductors and directors may work. Music teachers in schools often take on conducting as a natural extension of their duties. Conservatories and institutions of higher learning frequently have fine orchestras, choruses, and bands that often choose conductors from the faculty. There are numerous summer festivals that employ conductors, and conductors may also find positions with community orchestras and choruses, local opera companies, and musical theater groups; even amateur groups sometimes hire outside conductors. For the very exceptional, of course, there is the possibility of conducting with famous orchestras, theaters, and opera companies, as well as the musical groups associated with broadcasting and film studios. Well-known conductors are in demand and travel a great deal, appearing as guest conductors with other orchestras or making personal appearances.

Starting Out

A career in conducting begins with a sound musical education. Working as an instrumentalist in an orchestral group under a good conductor whose technique can be studied is an important step toward conducting. The piano is an important instrument for the conductors to know, because it will not only enable them to score and arrange more easily, it also will be useful in coaching singers, which many conductors do as a sideline, and in rehearsing an orchestra as assistant conductor. That is not to say, however, that other instrumentalists do not also acquire a good background for conducting.

With a solid foundation in musical education and some experience with an orchestra, young conductors should seek any way possible to acquire experience conducting. There are many grants and fellowships you can apply for, and many summer music festivals advertise for conductors. These situations often present the opportunity to work or study under a famous conductor who has been engaged to oversee or administer a festival. Such experience is invaluable because it provides opportunities to make contacts for various other conducting positions. These may include apprenticeships, jobs with university choirs and orchestras (which may include a faculty position), or opportunities with community orchestras, small opera companies, or amateur groups that seek a professional music director. Experience in these positions can lead to offers with major orchestras, operas, or musical theater companies as assistant or associate conductor.

Not everyone will want or be able to move into a major role as conductor of a well-known orchestra. Many, in fact most, will remain in other positions such as those described. Those seeking to further their career as a conductor may want to invest in a personal manager who will find bookings and situations for ambitious young talent. More than likely, entering the conducting field will take more of an investment than most other careers. Music education, applying for grants and fellowships, and attending workshops, summer music camps, and festivals can add up to a considerable expense. Moving into a good conducting job may take time as well, and young people going into the field should not expect to reach the pinnacle of their profession until they are well into their 30s or 40s or even older.

Advancement

There is no real hierarchy in an orchestra organization that one can climb to the role of conductor. The most likely advancement within an organization would be from the position of assistant or associate conductor or from that of the head first violinist, that is, the concertmaster. Conductors generally move from smaller conducting jobs to larger ones. A likely advancement would be from a small community orchestra or youth orchestra (probably a part-time position), to a small city orchestra (full- or part-time), and from there to a larger city orchestra, a mid-sized opera company, or directorship of a middle-level television or film company. Such advancement presumes that the conductor has had sufficient recognition and quality reviews to come to the attention of the larger musical groups.

Conductors who take the leadership of mid-sized city orchestras and opera companies may be in the hands of an agent or manager, who takes care of financial matters, guest bookings, and personal appearances. The agent will also be looking for advancement to more prestigious conducting jobs in the larger cities. At the point that conductors receive national or international recognition, it becomes a question of which major position they will accept as openings occur. It is unlikely that a major city orchestra would promote someone within the organization when the conductorship is open. It is more probable that a search committee will conduct an international search to find a "big name" conductor for the post. Conductors themselves can advance to top-level administrative positions, such as *artistic director* or *executive director.*

Earnings

The range of earnings for music conductors and directors is enormous, and there is variation from one category of conductors to another. For instance, many conductors work only part-time and make quite small yearly incomes for their conducting endeavors. Part-time choir directors for churches and temples, for instance, make from $3,500 to $25,000 per year, while full-time directors make from $15,000 to $40,000 per year. Conductors of dance bands make from $300 to $1,200 per week. Opera and choral group conductors make as little as $8,000 per year working part-time at the community level, but salaries range to over $100,000 per year for those with permanent positions with established companies in major cities. The same applies to symphony orchestra conductors who, for instance, make $25,000 to $40,000 per year conducting smaller, regional orchestras, but who can make $500,000 or more a year if they become the resident conductor of an internationally famous orchestra.

Work Environment

The working conditions of conductors range as widely as their earnings. The conductors of small musical groups at the community level may rehearse in a member's basement, a community center, a high school gym, or in a church or temple. Performances may be held in some of those same places. Lighting, heating or cooling, sound equipment, and musical instrument quality may all be less than adequate. On the other hand, conductors of major orchestras in the larger metropolitan centers usually have ideal working conditions, generally having the same outstanding facilities for rehearsal and performance. Many universities, colleges, and conservatories, even some of the smaller ones, also have state-of-the-art facilities.

Outlook

The operating cost for an orchestra continues to grow every year, and music organizations are in constant budget-trimming modes as have been most other professional business organizations in the last decade. This has tended to affect growth in the orchestra field and, accordingly, the number of conducting jobs. Additionally, the overall number of orchestras in the United States has grown only slightly in the last two decades. The number of orchestras in academia declined slightly while community, youth, and city orchestras for the most part increased slightly in number. The slight growth pattern of orchestra groups will not nearly accommodate the number of people who graduated from music school during that period and are trying to become conductors. The competition for music conductor and director jobs, already tight, will become even tighter in the next decade. Only the most talented people moving into the field will be able to find full-time jobs.

For More Information

The following organizations provide information on career and internship opportunities.

American Federation of Musicians of the United States and Canada
Paramount Building
1501 Broadway, Suite 600
New York, NY 10036
Tel: 212-869-1330
Web: http://www.afm.org

American Guild of Musical Artists
1727 Broadway
New York, NY 10019
Tel: 212-265-3687
Email: AGMA@musicalartists.org
Web: http://www.musicalartists.org

American Symphony Orchestra League
33 West 60th Street, 5th Floor
New York, NY 10023-7905
Tel: 212-262-5161
Email: league@symphony.org
Web: http://www.symphony.org

Conductors' Guild, Inc.
North Lakeside Cultural Center
6219 North Sheridan Road
Chicago, IL 60660-1729
Tel: 773-764-7563
Email: guild@conductorsguild.net
Web: http://www.conductorsguild.org

Orchestras Canada
56 The Esplanade, Suite 311
Toronto, ON M5E 1A7 Canada
Tel: 416-366-8834
Email: info@oc.ca
Web: http://www.oc.ca

Musical Instrument Repairers and Tuners

Music Technical/shop	School Subjects
Artistic Mechanical/manipulative	Personal Skills
Primarily indoors One location with some travel	Work Environment
Some postsecondary training	Minimum Education Level
$15,000 to $31,408 to $65,458+	Salary Range
Voluntary for certain positions	Certification or Licensing
More slowly than the average	Outlook

Overview

Musical instrument repairers and tuners work on a variety of instruments, often operating inside music shops or repair shops to keep the pieces in tune and in proper condition. Those who specialize in working on pianos or pipe organs may travel to the instrument's location to work. Instrument repairers and tuners usually specialize in certain families of musical instruments, such as stringed or brass instruments. Depending on the instrument, they may be skilled in working with wood, metal, electronics, or other materials. There are approximately 8,000 of these workers employed in the United States.

History

The world's first musical instrument was the human body. Paleolithic dancers clapped, stamped, chanted, and slapped their bodies to mark rhythm. Gourd rattles, bone whistles, scrapers, hollow branch, and conch shell "trumpets," wooden rhythm pounders and knockers, and bullroarers followed. By the early Neolithic times, people had developed drums that produced two or more pitches and pottery and cane flutes that gave several notes. The musical bow, a primitive stringed instrument and forerunner of the jaw harp, preceded the bow-shaped harp (about 3000 BC) and the long-necked lute (about 2000 BC).

The history of the pipe organ stretches back to the third century BC, when the Egyptians developed an organ that used water power to produce a stream of air. A few centuries later, organs appeared in Byzantium that used bellows (a device that draws air in and then expels it with great force) to send air through the organ pipes. From that time until about AD 1500 all the features of the modern pipe organ were developed.

The first version of the violin, played by scraping a taut bow across several stretched strings, appeared in Europe around the year 1510. The end of the 16th century saw the development of the violin as it is known today. Over the next hundred years, violin making reached its greatest achievements in the area around Cremona, Italy, where families of master craftsmen, such as the Stradivaris, the Guarneris, and the Amatis, set a standard for quality that never has been surpassed. Today, their violins are coveted by players around the world for their tonal quality.

The modern piano is the end product of a gradual evolution from plucked string instruments, such as the harp, to instruments employing hammers of one kind or another to produce notes by striking the strings. By the late 1700s, the immediate ancestor of the modern piano had been developed. Improvements and modifications (most involving new materials or manufacturing processes) took place throughout the 19th century, resulting in today's piano.

In addition to the stringed instruments, contemporary orchestral instruments also include the woodwind, brass, and percussion families. Woodwinds include the flute, clarinet, oboe, bassoon, and saxophone. Brass instruments include the French horn, trumpet, cornet, trombone, and tuba. All require some professional care and maintenance at some time. The modern electronic organ is a descendent of the pipe organ. In 1934, Laurens Hammond, an American inventor, patented the first practical electronic organ, an instrument that imitates the sound of the pipe organ but requires much less space and is more economical and practical to own and operate. The development of electronic and computer technology produced the first synthesizers and synthesized instruments, which are used widely today.

The Job

All but the most heavily damaged instruments usually can be repaired by competent, experienced craftsworkers. In addition, instruments require regular maintenance and inspection to ensure that they play properly and to prevent small problems from becoming major ones.

Stringed-instrument repairers perform extremely detailed and difficult work. The repair of violins, violas, and cellos might be considered the finest woodworking done in the world today. Because their sound quality is so beautiful, some older, rarer violins are worth millions of dollars, and musicians will sometimes fly halfway around the world to have rare instruments repaired by master restorers. In many ways, the work of these master craftspeople may be compared to the restoration of fine art masterpieces.

When a violin or other valuable stringed instrument needs repair, its owner takes the instrument to a repair shop, which may employ many repairers. If the violin has cracks in its body, it must be taken apart. The pieces of a violin are held together by a special glue that allows the instrument to be dismantled easily for repair purposes. The glue, which is made from hides and bones and has been used for more than 400 years, is sturdy but does not bond permanently with the wood.

To repair a crack in the back of a violin, the repairer first pops the back off the instrument. After cleaning the crack with warm water, the repairer glues the crack and attaches cleats or studs above the crack on the inside to prevent further splitting. The repairer reassembles the violin and closes the outside of the crack with fill varnish. Lastly, the repairer treats the crack scrupulously with retouch varnish so that it becomes invisible.

The repairer does not complete every step immediately after the previous one. Depending on the age and value of the instrument, a repair job can take three weeks or longer. Glues and varnishes need to set, and highly detailed work demands much concentration. The repairer also needs to do research to isolate the original type of varnish on the instrument and match it precisely with modern materials. The repairer usually has more than one repair job going at any one time.

A major restoration, such as the replacement of old patchwork or the fitting of inside patches to support the instrument, requires even more time. A large project can take two years or longer. A master restorer can put two thousand or more hours into the repair of a valuable violin that has nothing more than a few cracks in its finish. Since many fine instruments are worth two million dollars or more, they need intense work to preserve the superior quality of their sound. The repairer cannot rush the work, must concentrate on every detail, and complete the repair properly or risk other problems later on.

While all instruments are not made by Stradivari, they still need to be kept in good condition to be played well. Owners bring in their violins, violas, and cellos to the repair shop every season for cleaning, inspecting joints, and gluing gaps. The work involves tools similar to woodworker's tools, such as carving knives, planes, and gouges. The violin repairer will often need to play the instrument to check its condition and tune it. *Bow rehairers* maintain the quality of the taut, vibrating horsehair string that is stretched from end to end of the resilient wooden bow.

Wind-instrument repairers require a similar level of skill to that required of stringed-instrument repairers. However, the quality of sound is more standard among manufacturers, old instruments do not necessarily play any better than new ones, and these instruments do not command the same value as a fine violin.

The repairer first needs to determine the extent of repairs that the instrument warrants. The process may range from a few minor repairs to bring the instrument up to "playing condition" to a complete overhaul. After fixing the instrument, the repairer also will clean both the inside and outside and may replate the metal finish on a scuffed or rusty instrument.

For woodwinds such as clarinets and oboes, common repairs include fixing or replacing the moving parts of the instrument, including replacing broken keys with new keys, cutting new padding or corks to replace worn pieces, and replacing springs. If the body of the woodwind is cracked in any sections, the repairer will take the instrument apart and attempt to pin or glue the crack shut. In some situations, the repairer will replace the entire section or joint of the instrument.

Repairing brass instruments such as trumpets and French horns requires skill in metal working and plating. The pieces of these instruments are held together by solder, which the repairer must heat and remove to take the instrument apart for repair work. To fix dents, the repairer will unsolder the piece and work the dent out with hammers and more delicate tools and seal splits in the metal with solder as well. A final buffing and polishing usually removes any evidence of the repair.

If one of the valves of the brass instrument is leaking, the repairer may replate it and build up layers of metal to fill the gaps. At times, the repairer will replace a badly damaged valve with a new valve from the instrument manufacturer, but often the owner will discard the entire instrument because the cost of making a new valve from raw materials is prohibitive. Replacement parts are usually available from the manufacturer, but parts for older instruments are sometimes difficult or impossible to find. For this reason, many repairers save and stockpile discarded instruments for their parts.

Piano technicians and *piano tuners* repair and tune pianos so that when a key is struck, it will produce its correctly pitched note of the musical scale. A piano may go out of tune for a variety of reasons, including strings that have stretched or tightened from age, temperature change, relocation, or through use. Tuners use a special wrench to adjust the pins that control the tension on the strings. Piano tuners usually are specially trained for such work, but piano technicians also may perform it in connection with a more thorough inspection or overhaul of an instrument.

A piano's performance is also affected by problems in any of the thousands of moving parts of the action or by problems in the sounding board or the frame holding the strings. These are problems that the technician is trained to analyze and correct. They may involve replacing or repairing parts or making adjustments that will enable the existing parts to function more smoothly.

The life of a piano—that is, the period of time before it can no longer be properly tuned or adjusted to correct operational problems—is usually estimated at 20 years. Because the harp and strong outer wooden frame are seldom damaged, technicians often rebuild pianos by replacing the sounding board and strings, refurbishing and replacing parts where necessary, and refinishing the outer case.

In all their work, from tuning to rebuilding, piano technicians discover a piano's problems by talking to the owner and playing the instrument themselves. They may dismantle a piano partially on-site to determine the amount of wear to its parts and look for broken parts. They use common hand tools such as hammers, screwdrivers, and pliers. To repair and rebuild pianos, they use a variety of specialized tools for stringing and setting pins.

For *pipe organ technicians,* the largest part of the job is repairing and maintaining existing organs. This primarily involves tuning the pipes, which can be time consuming, even in a moderate-sized organ.

To tune a flue pipe, the technician moves a slide that increases or decreases the length of the "speaking" (note-producing) part of the pipe, varying its pitch. The technician tunes a reed pipe varying the length of the brass reed inside the pipe.

To tune an organ, the technician tunes either the "A" or "C" pipes by matching their notes with those of a tuning fork or electronic note-producing device. He or she then tunes the other pipes in harmony with the "A" or "C" notes. This may require a day or more for a moderate-sized organ and much longer for a giant concert organ.

Pipe organ technicians also diagnose, locate, and correct problems in the operating parts of the organ and perform preventive maintenance on a regular basis. To do this, they work with electric wind-generating equipment and with slides, valves, keys, air channels, and other equipment that enables the organist to produce the desired music.

Occasionally, a new organ is installed in a new or existing structure. Manufacturers design and install the largest organs. Each is unique, and the designer carefully supervises its construction and installation. Often, designers individually create moderate-sized organs specifically for the structure, usually churches, in which they will be played. Technicians follow the designer's blueprints closely during installation. The work involves assembling and connecting premanufactured components, using a variety of hand and power tools. Technicians may work in teams, especially when installing the largest pipes of the organ.

Although the electronic organ imitates the sound of the pipe organ, the workings of the two instruments have little in common. The electronic organ consists of electrical and electronic components and circuits that channel electrical current through various oscillators and amplifiers to produce sound when a player presses each key. It is rare for an oscillator or other component to need adjustment in the way an organ pipe needs to be adjusted to tune it. A technician tunes an electronic organ by testing it for electronic malfunction and replacing or repairing the component, circuit board, or wire.

The work of the *electronic organ technician* is closer to that of the television repair technician than it is to that of the pipe organ technician. The technician often begins looking for the source of a problem by checking for loose wires and solder connections. After making routine checks, technicians consult wiring diagrams that enable them to trace and test the circuits of the entire instrument to find malfunctions. For instance, an unusual or irregular voltage in a circuit may indicate a problem. Once the problem has been located, the technician often solves it by replacing a malfunctioning part, such as a circuit board.

These technicians work with common electrician's tools: pliers, wire cutters, screwdriver, soldering iron, and testing equipment. Technicians can make most repairs and adjustments in the customer's home. Because each manufacturer's instruments are arranged differently, technicians follow manufacturers' wiring diagrams and service manuals to locate trouble spots and make repairs. In larger and more complex instruments, such as those in churches and theaters, this may require a day or more of searching and testing.

Other types of repairers work on a variety of less common instruments. *Percussion tuners and repairers* work on drums, bells, congas, timbales, cymbals, and castanets. They may stretch new skins over the instrument, replace broken or missing parts, or seal cracks in the wood.

Accordion tuners and repairers work on free-reed portable accordions, piano accordions, concertinas, harmoniums, and harmonicas. They repair leaks in the bellows of an instrument, replace broken or damaged reeds, and perform various maintenance tasks. Other specialists in instrument repair include fretted-instrument repairers, harp regulators, trombone-slide assemblers, metal-reed tuners, tone regulators, and chip tuners.

In addition to repair work, those who run their own music or repair shops perform duties similar to others in the retail business. They order stock from instrument manufacturers, wait on customers, handle their accounting and billing work, and perform other duties.

Requirements

High School

No matter what family of instruments interests you, you should start preparing for this field by gaining a basic knowledge of music. Take high school classes in music history, music theory, and choir, chorus, or other singing classes. By learning to read music, developing an ear for scales, and understanding tones and pitches, you will be developing an excellent background for this work. Also, explore your interest in instruments (besides your own voice) by taking band or orchestra classes or private music lessons. By learning how to play an instrument, you will also learn how a properly tuned and maintained instrument should sound. If you find yourself interested in instruments with metal parts, consider taking art or shop classes that provide the opportunity to do metal working. These classes will allow you to practice soldering and work with appropriate tools. If you are interested in piano or stringed instruments, consider taking art or shop classes that offer woodworking. In these classes you will learn finishing techniques and use tools that you may relate to the building and maintaining of the bodies of these instruments.

Because instrument repair of any type is precision work, you will benefit from taking mathematics classes such as algebra and geometry. Since many instrument repairers and tuners are self-employed, take business or accounting classes to prepare for this possibility. Finally, take English classes to develop your research, reading, and communication skills. You will often need to consult technical instruction manuals for repair and maintenance work. You will also need strong communication skills that will help you broaden your client base as well as help you explain to your clients what work needs to be done.

Postsecondary Training

There are two main routes to becoming a music instrument repairer and tuner: extensive apprenticeship or formal education through technical or vocational schools. Apprenticeships, however, can be difficult to find. You will simply need to contact instrument repair shops and request a position as a trainee. Once you have found a position, the training period may last from two to five years. You will get hands-on experience working with the instruments as well as having other duties around the shop, such as selling any products offered.

Depending on the family of instruments you want to work with, there are a number of technical or vocational schools that offer either courses or full-time programs in repair and maintenance work. Professional organizations may have information on such schools. The National Association of Professional Band Instrument Repair Technicians, for example, provides a listing of schools offering programs in band instrument repair. The Piano Technicians Guild has information on both full-time programs and correspondence courses. Wind-instrument repairers can learn their crafts at one of the handful of vocational schools in the country that offers classes in instrument repair. Entrance requirements vary among schools, but all require at least a high school diploma or GED. Typical classes that are part of any type of instrument repair and tuning education include acoustics, tool care and operation, and small business practices. Depending on what instrument you choose to specialize in, you may also study topics such as buffing, dent removal, plating, soldering, or woodworking. You may also be required to invest in personal hand tools and supplies, and you may need to make tools that are not available from suppliers.

If you are interested in working with electronic organs, you will need at least one year of electronics technical training to learn organ repair skills. Electronics training is available from community colleges and technical and vocational schools. The U.S. Armed Forces also offer excellent training in electronics, which you can apply to instrument work. Electronic organ technicians also may attend training courses offered by electronic organ manufacturers.

It is important to keep in mind that even those who take courses or attend school for their postsecondary training will need to spend years honing their skills.

A number of instrument repairers and tuners have completed some college work or have a bachelor's degree. A 1997 Piano Technicians Guild survey (the most recent statistics available), for example, showed that at least 50 percent of their members had bachelor's degrees or higher. Although there are no college degrees in instrument repair, people who major in some type of music performance may find this background adds to their understanding of the work.

Certification or Licensing

The Piano Technicians Guild helps its members improve their skills and keep up with developments in piano technology. Refresher courses and seminars in new developments are offered by local chapters, and courses offered by manufacturers are publicized in Guild publications. The Guild also administers a series of tests that can lead to certification as a Registered Piano Technician (RPT).

Other Requirements

Personal qualifications for people in this occupational group include keen hearing and eyesight, mechanical aptitude, and manual dexterity. They should be resourceful and able to learn on the job, because every instrument that needs repair is unique and requires individual care. Instrument repairers and tuners must also have the desire to learn throughout their professional lives. They expand their knowledge by studying trade magazines and manufacturers' service manuals related to new developments in their field. They may improve their skills in training programs and at regional and national seminars. Instrument manufacturers often offer training in the repair of their particular products.

Other qualifications for the instrument repairer and tuner are related to his or her instrument specialty. For example, the majority of piano technicians work in customers' homes, and they should be able to communicate clearly when talking about a piano's problems and when advising a customer. A pleasant manner and good appearance are important to instill confidence. While the physical strength required for moving a piano is not often needed, the technician may be required to bend or stand in awkward positions while working on the piano. Those interested in careers as pipe organ technicians need the ability to follow blueprints and printed instructions to plan and execute repair or installation work. And any repairer and tuner who works in a store selling musical instruments should be comfortable working with the public.

Exploring

One of the best ways to explore this field is to take some type of musical instrument lessons. This experience will help you develop an ear for tonal quality and acquaint you with the care of your instrument. It will also put you in contact with those who work professionally with music. You may develop a contact with someone at the store where you have purchased or rented your instrument, and, naturally, you will get to know your music teacher. Ask these people what they know about the repair and tuning business. Your high school or local college music departments can also be excellent places for meeting those who work with instruments. Ask teachers in these departments whom they know working in instrument repair. You may be able to set up an informational interview with a repairer and tuner you find through these contacts. Ask the repairer about his or her education, how he or she got interested in the work, what he or she would recommend for someone considering the field, and any other questions you may have.

Part-time and summer jobs that are related closely to this occupation may be difficult to obtain because full-time trainees usually handle the routine tasks of a helper. Nevertheless, it is worth applying for such work at music stores and repair shops in case they do not use full-time trainees. General clerical jobs in stores that sell musical instruments may help familiarize you with the language of the field and may offer you the opportunity to observe skilled repairers at work.

Employers

Approximately 8,000 people work as musical instrument repairers and tuners of all types in the United States. About one-fourth of this number are self-employed and may operate out of their own homes. The majority of the rest work in repair shops and music stores and for manufacturers. Large cities with extensive professional music activity, both in the United States and in Europe, are the best places of employment. Musical centers such as Chicago, New York, London, and Vienna are the hubs of the repair business for stringed instruments, and any repairer who wishes a sufficient amount of work may have to relocate to one of these cities.

Some piano technicians work in factories where pianos are made. They may assemble and adjust pianos or inspect the finished instruments. Some technicians work in shops that rebuild pianos. Many piano repairers and tuners work in customers' homes.

Most of the few hundred pipe organ technicians in the United States are self-employed. These pipe organ technicians are primarily engaged in repairing and tuning existing organs. A small number are employed by organ manufacturers and are engaged in testing and installing new instruments. The great expense involved in manufacturing and installing a completely new pipe organ decreases demand and makes this type of work scarce.

Starting Out

Vocational schools and community colleges that offer instrument repair training can usually connect recent graduates with repair shops that have job openings. Those who enter the field through apprenticeships work at the local shop where they are receiving their training. Professional organizations may also have information on job openings.

Advancement

Repairers and tuners may advance their skills by participating in special training programs. A few who work for large dealers or repair shops may move into supervisory positions.

Another path to advancement is to open one's own musical repair shop and service. Before doing this, however, the worker should have adequate training to survive the strong competition that exists in the tuning and repair business. In many cases, repairers may need to continue working for another employer until they develop a clientele large enough to support a full-time business.

A few restorers of stringed instruments earn worldwide reputations for their exceptional skill. Their earnings and the caliber of their customers both rise significantly when they become well known. It takes a great deal of hard work and talent to achieve such professional standing, however, and this recognition only comes after years in the field. At any one time, there may be perhaps 10 restorers in the world who perform exceptional work, while another hundred or so are known for doing very good work. The work of these few craftspeople is always in great demand.

Earnings

Wages vary depending on geographic area and the worker's specialty and skill. Full-time instrument repairers and tuners had a median income of about $31,408 in 2000, according to the U.S. Department of Labor. The highest paid 10 percent earned $65,458 or more per year. Some helpers work for the training they get and receive no pay. Repairers and tuners who are self-employed earn more than those who work for music stores or instrument manufacturers, but their income is generally less stable. Repairers who gain an international reputation for the quality of their work earn the highest income in this field.

Repairers and tuners working as employees of manufacturers or stores often receive some benefits, including health insurance, vacation days, and holiday and sick pay. Self-employed repairers and tuners must provide these for themselves.

Work Environment

Repairers and tuners work in shops, homes, and instrument factories, surrounded by the tools and materials of their trade. The atmosphere is somewhat quiet but the pace is often busy. Since repairers and tuners are usually paid by the piece, they have to concentrate and work diligently on their repairs. Piano technicians and tuners generally perform their work in homes, schools, churches, and other places where pianos are located.

Instrument tuners and repairers may work more than 40 hours a week, especially during the fall and winter, when people spend more time indoors playing musical instruments. Self-employed tuners and repairers often work evenings and weekends, when it is more convenient to meet with the customer.

As noted, many repairs demand extreme care and often long periods of time to complete. For large instruments, such as pianos and pipe organs, repairers and tuners may have to work in cramped locations for some length of time, bending, stretching, and using tools that require physical strength to handle. Tuning pianos and organs often requires many hours and can be tedious work.

The field at times may be very competitive, especially among the more prestigious repair shops for stringed instruments. Most people at the major repair shops know each other and vie for the same business. There is often a great deal of pressure from owners to fix their instruments as soon as possible, but a conscientious repairer cannot be rushed into doing a mediocre job.

In spite of these drawbacks, repair work is almost always interesting, challenging, and rewarding. Repairers never do the same job twice, and each instrument comes with its own set of challenges. The work requires repairers to call on their ingenuity, skill, and personal pride every day.

Outlook

Job opportunities for musical instrument repairers and tuners are expected to grow more slowly than the average through 2010, according to the U.S. Department of Labor. This is a small, specialized field, and replacement needs will be the source of most jobs. Because training positions and school programs are relatively difficult to find, those with thorough training and education will have the best employment outlook.

It is a luxury for most owners to have their instruments tuned and repaired, and they tend to postpone these services when money is scarce. Tuners and repairers therefore may lose income during economic downturns. In addition, few trainees are hired at repair shops or music stores when business is slow.

For More Information

For information on organ and choral music fields, contact:

American Guild of Organists/The American Organist Magazine
475 Riverside Drive, Suite 1260
New York, NY 10115
Tel: 212-870-2310
Email: info@agohq.org
Web: http://www.agohq.org

For information about electronic instrument repair, contact the following organizations:

Electronic Industries Alliance
2500 Wilson Boulevard
Arlington, VA 22201
Tel: 703-907-7790
Web: http://www.eia.org

Electronics Technicians Association
502 North Jackson Street
Greencastle, IN 46135
Tel: 800-288-3824
Email: eta@tds.net
Web: http://eta-sda.com

For information about instrument repair and a list of schools offering courses in the field, contact:

National Association of Professional Band Instrument Repair Technicians
PO Box 51
Normal, IL 61761
Tel: 309-452-4257
Email: chagler@napbirt.org
Web: http://www.napbirt.org

For information on certification, contact:

Piano Technicians Guild
3930 Washington
Kansas City, MO 64111-2963
Tel: 816-753-7747
Email: ptg@ptg.org
Web: http://www.ptg.org

Musicians

Overview

Musicians perform, compose, conduct, arrange, and teach music. Performing musicians may work alone or as part of a group, or ensemble. They may play before live audiences in clubs or auditoriums, or they may perform on television or radio, in motion pictures, or in a recording studio. Musicians usually play either classical, popular (including country), jazz, or folk music, but many musicians play several musical styles. Musicians, singers, and related workers hold about 240,000 jobs in the United States.

History

According to ancient art and artifacts, humankind has enjoyed music at least since the establishment of early civilizations in the Tigris-Euphrates Valley. Musicians of these early cultures played instruments that were blown, plucked, or struck, just as is done by the musicians of today. Most of the early music, however, was vocal. In the ancient Egyptian temples, choirs sang to honor the gods, while in the court, musicians accompanied their songs with instruments of the wind, string, and percussion families. The ancient tribes of Israel used a shofar (a ram's horn trumpet) to accompany some religious services, a practice that has been continued to the present day. It was the development of music in Greece, however, that clearly influenced Western music. The Greeks had a system of writing their music down, and they invented a system of scales called "modes" that was the forerunner of the modern major and minor scales. Roman music was founded on the Greek model. A seven-tone scale evolved under the Romans, and instrumentation was further developed, including the straight trumpet.

During the Middle Ages, a great catalyst for both change and preservation in music arrived with the development of musical notation, the written language of music. Much credit for this accomplishment is ascribed to Guido d'Arezzo, an 11th-century Italian monk who devised a system for writing music down on paper so that it might be preserved and later read and played by other musicians. Many monks during this period devoted their lives to the preservation of the music of the church, and much of the knowledge and development of music is owed to their dedicated efforts. Throughout the Middle Ages, singers and musicians traveled from town to town to play for new audiences. During the Renaissance, singers and musicians often had to depend on wealthy patrons for support. What we now call classical music developed during the Renaissance.

During the 17th century, the operatic form developed, most notably in Italy. Opera, combining orchestral music and theater with an extremely popular form of singing, opened up a whole new range of opportunities for musicians, particularly singers. Singers soon began to gain fame in their own right for their incredible vocal feats, and great public demand for their performances allowed them to sever their dependent ties to wealthy patrons.

From about the mid-18th century to the mid-19th century, opportunities for instrumental musicians expanded as composers began to write more complex musical pieces for larger ensembles. During this period, many of the world's great symphonies, concerti, and chamber music were written and performed by musicians playing an ever-widening array of instruments. In the early 1800s came the onset of the Romantic movement in music, in which composers wrote with a new degree of emotionalism and self-expression that conductors and musicians were expected to express in their performance. Around the beginning of the 20th century, musical performers faced another challenge as composers, seeking to break new musical ground, adapted atonal and discordant sounds and new rhythms to their compositions, a direction greatly influenced by the 12-tone scale of Arnold Schoenberg (1874-1951).

The operatic, classical, and nationalistic music of Europe was brought to America by the migrating Europeans. Throughout the early history of the country, virtually all of the music played was European in style. By the end of the 19th century, however, and through the 20th, musicians increasingly came to play music that was distinctly American in style and composition. At least one musical form, jazz, was entirely an American invention.

The development of popular music and the development of recorded music greatly increased opportunities for musicians. U.S. popular music and jazz influenced music throughout the world. Swing grew out of jazz, and "big" swing bands mushroomed all over the United States during the late 1930s, 1940s, and into the 1950s. Big bands diminished by the late 1950s as rising costs and new popular music styles, such as rhythm and blues and rock and roll, directed the move to smaller groups using electric and electronic instruments. With the advent of electronic mass media, the musical superstar was created, as millions of people at a time could hear and see musical performers. Although the mass electronic media created an enormous market for popular music, it has ironically limited the market for live performances by musicians. The demand for live musicians was also reduced by the widening use of advanced electronic instruments, such as the synthesizer, which itself can replace a whole band, and the DJ (disc jockey), who plays recorded music over highly sophisticated sound systems, replacing musicians at clubs and gatherings.

Until about the mid-1900s, musicians and singers were largely an exploited group who made little money for the use of their skills. The growth of organizations designed to protect performing artists has helped greatly to improve the lot of musicians. Particularly effective was the American Federation of Musicians, the musicians' union, which created a wage scale and oversaw the rights of musicians in recording, broadcasting, theater, and at any event in which musicians or their recordings are used. In some situations the union requires that live musicians be hired.

The Job

Instrumental musicians play one or more musical instruments, usually in a group and in some cases as featured soloists. Musical instruments are usually classified in several distinct categories according to the method by which they produce sound: strings (violins, cellos, basses, etc.), which make sounds by vibrations from bowing or plucking; woodwinds (oboes, clarinets, saxophones), which make sounds by air vibrations through reeds; brass (trumpets, French horns, trombones, etc.), which make sounds by air vibrations through metal; and percussion (drums, pianos, triangles), which produce sound by striking. Instruments can also be classified as electric or acoustic, especially in popular music. Synthesizers are another common instrument, and computer and other electronic technology increasingly is used for creating music. Like other instrumental musicians, *singers* use their own voice as an instrument to convey music. They aim to express emotion through lyric phrasing and characterization.

Musicians may play in symphony orchestras, dance bands, jazz bands, rock bands, country bands, or other groups or they might go it alone. Some musicians may play in recording studios either with their group or as a session player for a particular recording. Recordings are in the form of records, tapes, compact discs, and videotape cassettes. *Classical musicians* perform in concerts, opera performances, and chamber music concerts, and they may also play in theater orchestras, although theater music is not normally classical. The most talented ones may work as soloists with orchestras or alone in recitals. Some classical musicians accompany singers and choirs, and they may also perform in churches and temples.

Musicians who play popular music make heavy use of such rhythm instruments as piano, bass, drums, and guitar. *Jazz musicians* also feature woodwind and brass instruments, especially the saxophone and trumpet, and they extensively utilize the bass. Synthesizers are also commonly used instruments; some music is performed entirely on synthesizers, which can be programmed to imitate a variety of instruments and sounds. Musicians in jazz, blues, country, and rock groups play clubs, festivals, and concert halls and may perform music for recordings, television, and motion picture sound tracks. Occasionally they appear in a movie themselves. Other musicians compose, record, and perform entirely with electronic instruments, such as synthesizers and other devices. In the late 1970s, *rap artists* began using turntables as musical instruments, and later, samplers, which record a snippet of other songs and sounds, as part of their music.

Instrumental musicians and singers use their skills to convey the form and meaning of written music. They work to achieve precision, fluency, and emotion within a piece of music, whether through an instrument or through their own voice. Musicians practice constantly to perfect their techniques.

Many musicians supplement their incomes through teaching, while others teach as their full-time occupation, perhaps playing jobs occasionally. Voice and instrumental music teachers work in colleges, high schools, elementary schools, conservatories, and in their own studios; often they give concerts and recitals featuring their students. Many professional musicians give private lessons. Students learn to read music, develop their voices, breathe correctly, and hold their instruments properly.

Choral directors lead groups of singers in schools and other organizations. Church choirs, community oratorio societies, and professional symphony choruses are among the groups that employ choral directors outside of school settings. Choral directors audition singers, select music, and direct singers in achieving the tone, variety, intensity, and phrasing that they feel is required. *Orchestra conductors* do the same with instrumental musicians. Many work in schools and smaller communities, but the best conduct large orchestras in major cities. Some are resident instructors, while others travel constantly, making guest appearances with major national and foreign orchestras. They are responsible for the overall sound and quality of their orchestras.

Individuals also write and prepare music for themselves or other musicians to play and sing. *Composers* write the original music for symphonies, songs, or operas using musical notation to express their ideas through melody, rhythm, and harmony. *Arrangers* and *orchestrators* take a composer's work and transcribe it for the various orchestra sections or individual instrumentalists and singers to perform; they prepare music for film scores, musical theater, television, or recordings. *Copyists* assist composers and arrangers by copying down the various parts of a composition, each of which is played by a different section of the orchestra. *Librettists* write words to opera and musical theater scores, and *lyricists* write words to songs and other short musical pieces. A number of *songwriters* compose both music and lyrics, and many are musicians who perform their own songs.

Requirements

High School

If you are interested in becoming a musician, you will probably have begun to develop your musical skills long before you enter high school. While you are in high school, however, there are a number of classes you can take that will help you broaden your knowledge. Naturally, take band, orchestra, or choir classes depending on your interest. In addition, you should also take mathematics classes, since any musician needs to understand counting, rhythms, and beats. Many professional musicians write at least some of their own music, and a strong math background is very helpful for this. If your high school offers courses in music history or appreciation, be sure to take these. Finally, take classes that will improve your communication skills and your understanding of people and emotions, such as English and psychology. If you are interested in working in the classical music field, you will most likely need a college degree to succeed in this area. Therefore, be sure to round out your high school education by taking other college preparatory classes. Finally, no matter what type of musician you want to be, you will need to devote much of your after-school time to your private study and practice of music.

Postsecondary Training

Depending on your interest, especially if it is popular music, further formal education is not required. College or conservatory degrees are only required for those who plan to teach in institutions. Nevertheless, you will only benefit from continued education.

Scores of colleges and universities have excellent music schools, and there are numerous conservatories that offer degrees in music. Many schools have noted musicians on their staff, and music students often have the advantage of studying under a professor who has a distinguished career in music. By studying with someone like this, you will not only learn more about music and performance, but you will also begin to make valuable connections in the field. You should know that having talent and a high grade point average do not always ensure entry into the top music schools. Competition for positions is extremely tough. You will probably have to audition, and only the most talented are accepted.

College undergraduates in music school will generally take courses in music theory, harmony, counterpoint, rhythm, melody, ear training, applied music, and music history. Courses in composing, arranging, and conducting are available in most comprehensive music schools. Students will also have to take courses such as English and psychology along with a regular academic program.

Certification or Licensing

Musicians who want to teach in state elementary and high schools must be state certified. To obtain a state certificate, musicians must satisfactorily complete a degree-granting course in music education at an institution of higher learning. About 600 institutions in the United States offer programs in music education that qualify students for state certificates. Music education programs include many of the same courses mentioned earlier for musicians in general. They also would include education courses and supervised practice teaching. To teach in colleges and universities or in conservatories generally requires a graduate degree in music. Widely recognized musicians, however, sometimes receive positions in higher education without having obtained a degree.

The American Guild of Organists offers a number of voluntary, professional certifications to its members. Visit the Guild's Web site (contact information at the end of this article) for more information.

Other Requirements

Hard work and dedication are key factors in a musical career, but music is an art form, and like those who practice any of the fine arts, musicians will succeed according to the amount of musical talent they have. Those who have talent and are willing to make sacrifices to develop it are the ones most likely to succeed. How much talent and ability one has is always open to speculation and opinion, and it may take years of studying and practice before musicians can assess their own degree of limitation.

There are other requirements necessary to becoming a professional musician that are just as important as training, education, and study. Foremost among these is a love of music strong enough to endure the arduous training and working life of a musician. To become an accomplished musician and to be recognized in the field requires an uncommon degree of dedication, self-discipline, and drive. Musicians who would move ahead must practice constantly with a determination to improve their technique and quality of performance. Musicians also need to develop an emotional toughness that will help them deal with rejection, indifference to their work, and ridicule from critics, which will be especially prevalent early in their careers. There is also praise and adulation along the way, which is easier to take but also requires a certain psychological handling.

For musicians interested in careers in popular music, little to no formal training is necessary. Many popular musicians teach themselves to play their instruments, which often results in the creation of new and exciting playing styles. Quite often, popular musicians do not even know how to read music. Some would say that many rock musicians do not even know how to play their instruments. This was especially true in the early days of the punk era. Most musicians, however, have a natural talent for rhythm and melody.

Many musicians often go through years of "paying their dues"—that is, receiving little money, respect, or attention for their efforts. Therefore, they must have a strong sense of commitment to their careers and to their creative ideas.

Professional musicians generally hold membership in the American Federation of Musicians (AFL-CIO), and concert soloists also hold membership in the American Guild of Musical Artists, Inc. (AFL-CIO). Singers can belong to a branch of Associated Actors and Artists of America (AFL-CIO). Music teachers in schools often hold membership in MENC: The National

Association for Music Education (formerly Music Educators National Conference).

Exploring

The first step to exploring your interest in a musical career is to become involved with music. Elementary schools, high schools, and institutions of higher education all present a number of options for musical training and performance, including choirs, ensembles, bands, and orchestras. You also may have chances to perform in school musicals and talent shows. Those involved with services at churches, synagogues, or other religious institutions have excellent opportunities for exploring their interest in music. If you can afford to, take private music lessons.

Besides learning more about music, you will most likely have the chance to play in recitals arranged by your teacher. You may also want to attend special summer camps or programs that focus on the field. Interlochen Center for the Arts, for example, offers summer camps for students from the elementary to the high school level. College, university, and conservatory students gain valuable performance experience by appearing in recitals and playing in bands, orchestras, and school shows. The more enterprising students in high school and in college form their own bands and begin earning money by playing while still in school.

It is important for you to take advantage of every opportunity to audition so that you become comfortable with this process. There are numerous community amateur and semiprofessional theater groups throughout the United States that produce musical plays and operettas, in which beginning musicians can gain playing experience.

Employers

Most musicians work in large urban areas and are particularly drawn to the major recording centers, such as Chicago, New York City, Los Angeles, Nashville, and Miami Beach. Most musicians find work in churches, temples, schools, clubs, restaurants, and cruise lines, at weddings, in opera and ballet productions, and on film, television, and radio. Religious organizations are the largest single source of work for musicians.

Full-time positions as a musician in a choir, symphony orchestra, or band are few and are held only by the most talented. Musicians who are versatile and willing to work hard will find a variety of opportunities available, but all musicians should understand that work is not likely to be steady or provide much security. Many musicians support themselves in another line of work while pursuing their musical careers on a part-time basis. Busy musicians often hire agents to find employers and negotiate contracts or conditions of employment.

Starting Out

Young musicians need to enter as many playing situations as they can in their school and community musical groups. They should audition as often as possible, because experience at auditioning is very important. Whenever possible, they should take part in seminars and internships offered by orchestras, colleges, and associations. The National Orchestral Association offers training programs for musicians who want a career in the orchestral field.

Musicians who want to perform with established groups, such as choirs and symphony orchestras, enter the field by auditioning. Recommendations from teachers and other musicians often help would-be musicians obtain the opportunity to audition. Concert and opera soloists are also required to audition. Musicians must prepare themselves thoroughly for these auditions, which are demanding and stressful. A bad audition can be very discouraging for the young musician.

Popular musicians often begin playing at low-paying social functions and at small clubs or restaurants. If people like their performances, they usually move on to bookings at larger rooms in better clubs. Continued success leads to a national reputation and possible recording contracts. Jazz musicians tend to operate in the same way, taking every opportunity to audition with established jazz musicians.

Music teachers enter the field by applying directly to schools. College and university placement offices often have listings of positions. Professional associations frequently list teaching openings in their newsletters and journals, as do newspapers. Music-oriented journals such as the American Federation of Musicians' journal, *International Musician,* are excellent sources to check for job listings.

Advancement

Popular musicians, once they have become established with a band, advance by moving up to more famous bands or by taking leadership of their own group. Bands may advance from playing small clubs to larger halls and even stadiums and festivals. They may receive a recording contract; if their songs or recordings prove successful, they can command higher fees for their contracts. Symphony orchestra musicians advance by moving to the head of their section of the orchestra. They can also move up to a position such as assistant or associate conductor. Once instrumental musicians acquire a reputation as accomplished artists, they receive engagements that are of higher status and remuneration, and they may come into demand as soloists. As their reputations develop, both classical and popular musicians may receive attractive offers to make recordings and personal appearances.

Popular and opera singers move up to better and more lucrative jobs through recognition of their talent by the public or by music producers and directors and agents. Their advancement is directly related to the demand for their talent and their own ability to promote themselves.

Music teachers in elementary and secondary schools may, with further training, aspire to careers as supervisors of music of a school system, a school district, or an entire state. With further graduate training, teachers can qualify for positions in colleges, universities, and music conservatories, where they can advance to become department heads. Well-known musicians can become artists-in-residence in the music departments of institutions of higher learning.

Earnings

It is difficult to estimate the earnings of the average musician, because what a musician earns is dependent upon his or her skill, reputation, geographic location, type of music, and number of engagements per year.

According to the American Federation of Musicians, musicians in the major U.S. symphony orchestras earned salaries of between $24,720 and $100,196 during the 2000-01 performance season. The season for these major orchestras, generally located in the largest U.S. cities, ranges from 24 to 52 weeks. Featured musicians and soloists can earn much more, especially those with an international reputation. According to the *Occupational Outlook Handbook,* median annual earnings of musicians, singers, and related workers were $36,740 in 2000.

Popular musicians are usually paid per concert or "gig." A band just starting out playing a small bar or club may be required to play three sets a night, and each musician may receive next to nothing for the entire evening. Often, bands receive a percentage of the cover charge at the door. Some musicians play for drinks alone. On average, however, pay per musician ranges from $30 to $300 or more per night. Bands that have gained a recognition and a following may earn far more, because a club owner can usually be assured that many people will come to see the band play. The most successful popular musicians, of course, can earn millions of dollars each year. By the end of the 1990s, some artists, in fact, had signed recording contracts worth $20 million or more.

Musicians are well paid for studio recording work, when they can get it. For recording film and television background music, musicians are paid a minimum of about $185 for a three-hour session; for record company recordings they receive a minimum of about $235 for three hours. Instrumentalists performing live earn anywhere from $30 to $300 per engagement, depending on their degree of popularity, talent, and the size of the room they play.

According to the American Guild of Organists, full-time organists employed by religious institutions had the following base salary ranges by educational attainment in 2002: bachelor's degree, $35,285-$46,463; master's degree, $40,145-$53,610; and Ph.D., $45,225-$60,346.

The salaries received by music teachers in public elementary and secondary schools are the same as for other teachers. According to the U.S. Department of Labor, public elementary school and high school teachers had median yearly earnings of $41,820 in 1999-2000. Music teachers in colleges and universities have widely ranging salaries. Most teachers supplement their incomes through private instruction and by performing in their off hours.

Most musicians do not, as a rule, work steadily for one employer, and they often undergo long periods of unemployment between engagements. Because of these factors, few musicians can qualify for unemployment compensation. Unlike other workers, most musicians also do not enjoy such benefits as sick leave or paid vacations. Some musicians, on the other hand, who work under contractual agreements, do receive benefits, which usually have been negotiated by artists unions, such as the American Federation of Musicians.

Work Environment

Work conditions for musicians vary greatly. Performing musicians generally work in the evenings and on weekends. They also spend much time practicing and rehearsing for performances. Their workplace can be almost anywhere, from a swanky club to a high school gymnasium to a dark, dingy bar. Many concerts are given outdoors and in a variety of weather conditions. Performers may be given a star's dressing room, share a mirror in a church basement, or have to change in a bar's storeroom. They may work under the hot camera lights of film or television sets or tour with a troupe in subzero temperatures. They may work amid the noise and confusion of a large rehearsal of a Broadway show or in the relative peace and quiet of a small recording studio. Seldom are two days in a performer's life just alike.

Many musicians and singers travel a great deal. More prominent musicians may travel with staffs who make their arrangements and take care of wardrobes and equipment. Their accommodations are usually quite comfortable, if not luxurious, and they are generally playing in major urban centers. Lesser-known musicians may have to take care of all their own arrangements and put up with modest accommodations in relatively remote places. Some musicians perform on the streets, in subway tunnels, and other places likely to have a great deal of passersby. Symphony orchestra musicians probably travel less than most, but those of major orchestras usually travel first-class.

The chief characteristic of musical employment is its lack of continuity. Few musicians work full-time and most experience periods of unemployment between engagements. Most work day jobs to supplement their music or performing incomes. Those who are in great demand generally have agents and managers to help direct their careers.

Music teachers affiliated with institutions work the same hours as other classroom teachers. Many of these teachers, however, spend time after school and on weekends directing and instructing school vocal and instrumental groups. Teachers may also have varied working conditions. They may teach in a large urban school, conducting five different choruses each day, or they may work in several rural elementary schools and spend much time driving from school to school.

College or university instructors may divide their time between group and individual instruction. They may teach several musical subjects and may be involved with planning and producing school musical events. They may also supervise student music teachers when they do their practice teaching.

Private music teachers work part- or full-time out of their own homes or in separate studios. The ambiance of their workplace would be in accordance with the size and nature of their clientele.

Outlook

It is difficult to make a living solely as a musician, and this will continue because competition for jobs will be as intense as it has been in the past. Most musicians must hold down other jobs while pursuing their music careers. Thousands of musicians are all trying to "make it" in the music industry. Musicians are advised to be as versatile as possible, playing various kinds of music and more than one instrument. More importantly, they must be committed to pursuing their craft.

The U.S. Department of Labor predicts that employment of musicians will grow about as fast as the average through 2010. The demand for musicians will be greatest in theaters, bands, and restaurants as the public continues to spend more money on recreational activities. The outlook is favorable in churches and other religious organizations. The increasing numbers of cable television networks and new television programs will likely cause an increase in employment for musicians. The number of record companies has grown dramatically over the last decade, particularly among small, independent houses. Digital recording technology has also made it easier and less expensive for musicians to produce and distribute their own recordings. However, few musicians will earn substantial incomes from these efforts. Popular musicians may receive many short-term engagements in nightclubs, restaurants, and theaters, but these engagements offer little job stability. The supply of musicians for virtually all types of music will continue to exceed the demand for the foreseeable future.

The opportunities for careers in teaching music are expected to grow at an average rate in elementary schools and in colleges and universities but at a slower rate in secondary schools. Although increasing numbers of colleges and universities are offering music programs, enrollments in schools at all levels have been depressed and are not expected to increase immediately. Some public schools facing severe budget problems have eliminated music programs altogether, making competition for jobs at that level even keener. In addition, private music teachers are facing greater competition from instrumental musicians who increasingly must turn to teaching because of the oversupply of musicians seeking playing jobs. Job availability is also diminishing because of the advent of electronic instruments such as synthesizers, which can replace a whole band, and the increasing trend to use recorded music.

For More Information

This union offers information on job opportunities, news about developments in the music field, and the journal, International Musician.

American Federation of Musicians of the United States and Canada
Paramount Building
1501 Broadway, Suite 600
New York, NY 10036
Tel: 212-869-1330
Web: http://www.afm.org

AGMA's Web site has information on upcoming auditions, news announcements for the field, and membership information.

American Guild of Musical Artists (AGMA)
1727 Broadway
New York, NY 10019
Tel: 212-265-3687
Email: AGMA@MusicalArtists.org
Web: http://www.musicalartists.org

For information on music summer camps program, contact:

Interlochen Center for the Arts
PO Box 199
Interlochen, MI 49643
Tel: 231-276-7200
Web: http://www.interlochen.org

This organization supports public outreach programs, promotes music education, and offers information on the career of music teacher.

MENC: The National Association for Music Education
1806 Robert Fulton Drive
Reston, VA 20191
Tel: 800-336-3768
Web: http://www.menc.org

MTNA' s Web site has information on competitions for music students.

Music Teachers National Association (MTNA)
Carew Tower
441 Vine Street, Suite 505
Cincinnati, OH 45202-2811
Tel: 513-421-1420
Email: mtnanet@mtna.org
Web: http://www.mtna.org

NASM is an organization of schools, colleges, and universities that provide music education. Visit the Web site for a listing of NASM-accredited institutions.

National Association of Schools of Music (NASM)
11250 Roger Bacon Drive, Suite 21
Reston, VA 20190
Tel: 703-437-0700
Email: info@arts-accredit.org
Web: http://www.arts-accredit.org/nasm/nasm.htm

For career information, contact:

National Orchestral Association
575 Lexington Avenue
New York, NY 10022
Tel: 212-350-4676
Email: noa@mindspring.com

This organization offers networking opportunities, career information, and a mentoring program.

Women In Music National Network
31121 Mission Boulevard, Suite 300
Hayward, CA 94544
Tel: 510-232-3897
Web: http://www.womeninmusic.com

Pop/Rock Musicians

	School Subjects
Business Music	
	Personal Skills
Artistic Communication/ideas	
	Work Environment
Indoors and outdoors Primarily multiple locations	
	Minimum Education Level
High school diploma	
	Salary Range
$25 to $25,000 to $1,000,000+	
	Certification or Licensing
None available	
	Outlook
About as fast as the average	

Overview

Pop/rock musicians perform in nightclubs, concert halls, on college campuses, and at live events such as festivals and fairs. They also record their music for distribution on CDs and audio cassettes. A pop/rock musician usually performs as a member of a band comprised of instrumentalists and vocalists. The band may perform original music or music composed and recorded by other artists or a combination of both.

History

Since the term "rock 'n' roll" was first coined by radio disc jockey Alan Freed in the 1950s, rock music has been a significant part of teenage culture. Rock music has always been marketed to teens, purchased by teens, and stirred controversy with parents. Though much of rock music has appealed to all ages, it was the teen culture that evolved in the 1950s that brought the doo wop and boogie woogie music of the South to audiences all across the country. Teens, for the first time in U.S. history, were spending their own money, and they were spending it on the records they heard spun on the radio. What had previously been music appreciated primarily by black audiences, was brought to white audiences by the success of Chuck Berry, Little Richard, and Fats Domino; then, later, Elvis Presley and Jerry Lee Lewis.

To capitalize on this popularity, recording companies hired songwriters, singers, and musicians to produce rock songs for the masses. Girl groups, such as the Ronettes, were formed in the 1960s. Later that decade, rock took on more diverse sounds, as Motown artists, the Beatles, and other performers experimented with the genre. Though this experimentation led to a variety of musical forms in the 1970s, including folk, heavy metal, disco, and punk, record sales slipped, but not for long. The 1980s saw the huge popularity of the music video and MTV, a cable network that brought music back to the teen culture and revived the music industry.

By the 1990s several networks had followed MTV's example, broadcasting music videos, concerts, and interviews with stars, along with other programming focused on music. And, as in the past, musical styles continued to develop. "Grunge," a sound that drew on classical rock as well as punk music and included an attitude opposing mainstream culture, began with a number of bands mainly from the Seattle area. Nirvana and Pearl Jam eventually became two of the leading groups associated with grunge music that gained national and international popularity. Rap, a style of music in which rhyming lyrics are said over music, and hip hop, which includes saying lyrics over music in addition to the sounds produced when records are intentionally scratched in certain ways, also became nationally popular during this decade although their roots can be traced back as far as the 1970s. Other music styles popular in the 1990s and 2000s and that began their development in earlier decades include industrial, house, and techno music.

The Job

The lives and lifestyles of pop and rock stars—the limousines, the groupies, and the multimillion-dollar record deals—are popular subjects for magazines, TV entertainment shows, and even movies. Though most pop and rock musicians do long for this kind of success, many, in reality, have careers that are far less glamorous and far less financially rewarding. Nevertheless, for those who are devoted to their music, this work can be extremely fulfilling. Pop and rock musicians don't need to live in a major city, have international tours, or record top-selling CDs in order to enjoy this career. Opportunities for this work exist across the country. According to the Recording Workshop, a school for the recording arts in Ohio, most cities of over 25,000 have at least one audio production studio. These studios cater to the many rock musicians writing songs, performing them, and promoting their music to regional and national audiences. Typically, rock and pop musicians have an interest in music while they are still young. They may learn to play an instrument, to sing, or to write music, and they begin to perform publicly, even if it's just for the neighborhood block party. Over time, with increasing skills and contacts in the field, they develop lives that involve performing music on a regular basis.

Julia Greenberg is a rock musician in New York who has devoted years to the pursuit of a career in the music industry. With her CD, *Past Your Eyes,* she's getting attention that should propel her to even greater success. "I started my own band, using all original music, in 1993," Greenberg says. "I hired musicians and old friends to arrange the songs to play on my first demo. I used the demo to get gigs at clubs." Her band was very well received, and she has managed to get gigs all around Manhattan ever since. She's played at clubs, such as Mercury Lounge, Fez, and Brownie's, that are famous for promoting new and established acts. "My music is in the singer/songwriter vein," she says. "I'm very much focused on the writing. But we're also a straight-ahead rock band." Her work is influenced by roots rock, as well as the New Wave music (Blondie, Elvis Costello) with which she grew up.

In order to be truly successful, rock and pop musicians need original material to perform. Some regional bands, however, do make careers for themselves by playing the music of famous bands, performing at local clubs, dances, wedding receptions, and private parties. They may specialize in a specific period of music, such as music of the 1980s or Motown hits of the 1960s. But A&R (artist and repertoire) coordinators for record companies, managers, producers, and other professionals in the recording industry are looking for musicians who write and perform their own music.

Pop and rock musicians must spend much time practicing their skills away from the stage. They work on writing music and lyrics, practicing their instruments, and practicing together as a band. Rehearsal time and commitment to the band are extremely important to these musicians. In order for the band to sound as good as it possibly can, all the instrumentalists and vocalists must develop a sense of each other's talents and styles. In order to promote their band, the members put together a tape (called a "demo") demonstrating their work and talent, which they then submit to club managers and music producers. When making a demo, or recording a CD for a record company, bands record in studios and work with recording professionals. Audio engineers, producers, and mixing engineers help to enhance the band's performance in order to make their music sound as good as it possibly can.

When booked by a club, the club's promotional staff may advertise a band's upcoming appearance. For the most part, however, bands that are not well known must do their own advertising. This can involve distributing flyers, sending press releases to area newspapers and arts weeklies, and sending announcements to those on their mailing list. A band's mailing list is composed of the names and addresses of people who have attended previous performances and have expressed interest in hearing about future gigs. Many bands also maintain Web sites listing their performance schedule. Of course, very successful pop and rock musicians have a well established fan base, and their record company or promoter handles all the advertising.

On the day of the performance, pop and rock groups arrive early to prepare the stage for their show. This involves setting up instruments and sound systems, checking for sound quality, and becoming familiar with the stage and facility. Together, the band goes over the list of songs to be performed.

The size, mood, and age of the audience will likely effect a group's performance. If they are playing to a small crowd in a club, they will probably have much more personal experiences (as they see individual audience members and gauge their reactions to songs), than when playing to an auditorium full of hundreds of people. If the audience is enthusiastic about the music, instead of simply waiting for the next band scheduled to appear, the musicians are likely to have a positive experience and perform well. Age of audience members is also a factor, because older crowds may have the opportunity to drink alcohol, which may make them less inhibited about being loud and showing their pleasure or displeasure over a performance. Regardless of the audience, however, professional musicians play each song to the best of their abilities, with the intention of entertaining and enlightening listeners and developing a strong base of devoted fans.

Requirements

High School

High school classes that will help you become a pop or rock musician include English, which will help you hone your writing abilities; business and mathematics, which will teach you basic business principles of budgeting and managing money; and, of course, music, specifically voice or instrument training. Playing in one or more of your high school bands will give you an idea of what it is like to interact with fellow musicians as well as perform in front of an audience.

Postsecondary Training

A college education isn't necessary for becoming a pop or rock musician, but it can help you learn about music, recording, and writing. In general, you should have a background in music theory and an understanding of a variety of styles of music. Learning to play one or more instruments, such as the piano or guitar, will be especially helpful in writing songs. You can pursue this education at a community college, university, or trade school. There are a number of seminars, conferences, and workshops available that will involve you with songwriting, audio recording, and producing.

Other Requirements

You need to be able to work closely with other artists and to have patience with the rehearsal and recording process. You'll also need persistence to proceed with your ambitions in the face of much rejection. "You have to have a really strong personality," Julia Greenberg says. "You have to be able to get up on stage and command a room. You have to be really starved for attention!"

Exploring

Talk to your music teachers at school about opportunities in music. Try to attend as many musical performances as possible; they don't all have to be in the pop/rock genre. Many clubs and other concert facilities offer all-ages shows where you can see musical artists perform firsthand. Depending on the size of the venue, you may have a chance to approach a musician after the show to ask a few questions about the field.

The best way to get experience is to learn to play an instrument or take voice lessons. Once you've mastered the basics, you can get together with friends or classmates and experiment with different musical styles. Don't forget the writing aspect of pop/rock music. Keep a journal of your thoughts and ideas. Read the lyrics of your favorite songs and try to figure out what makes them so appealing. Try to create the lyrics to a song of your own by combining this knowledge with your journal entries or other creative writing.

Employers

Some pop and rock musicians work for another member of the band who pays them to rehearse and perform. But in most cases, pop and rock musicians work on a freelance basis, taking on gigs as they come. Bands are hired to play at clubs, concert halls, and for community events. They may also play private gigs, weddings, and other celebrations. Many musicians also maintain flexible "day jobs" that help to support them as they perform on the evenings and weekends.

Starting Out

Many bands form when a group of friends get together to collaborate on the writing and performing of original songs. However, openings for band members are frequently advertised in the classifieds of local and college newspapers and arts weeklies. You may have to audition for many bands before you find one with which you fit, or you may have to put together your own group of musicians. If part of a new band, you'll have to put a lot of time into rehearsal, as well as gaining a following. This may involve playing a lot of shows for free until a club owner can rely on you to bring in a crowd.

Advancement

The sky's the limit when it comes to advancing in the music industry. Once musicians have made the right connections, they may find themselves with record deals, national concert dates, awards, and a great deal of media attention. Julia Greenberg dreams of success that will allow her to perform and write music full time. Through the help of independent investors, Greenberg has been able to finance a new demo. "I'm shopping the CD to industry people, and putting the CD out myself," she says. "A lot of people are doing this these days. Industry people are looking for artists who can get their own following." The music, available at http://www.cropduster.com, has already sparked a great deal of interest, including a write-up in *New York* magazine.

Earnings

Even professionals with regular club dates have difficulty predicting how much money they will earn from one year to the next. And for those just starting out, many will earn nothing as they play clubs and events for free in order to establish themselves on the music scene. Their goal may be simply to get paying shows where they can earn enough money to cover their expenses (for example, for travel and promotion). As groups become better known and can be relied on to draw an audience, they may be paid a percentage of a club's cover charge or drink receipts.

When playing for special occasions such as weddings, birthday parties, and bar mitzvahs, pop and rock groups can earn anything from a token amount, such as $25, to $1,000 or more once they have become well known in an area. While $1,000 might sound like a lot of money for a few hours of stage work, in reality the sum each musician gets will be much less. For example, if there are four members in the group, each will only receive $250—but this is before expenses and taxes. Once these have been figured in, each member may end up making less than $200. Now assume these musicians have fairly steady work and perform once almost every week for the year. At that rate, they would each be earning approximately $9,000 to $10,000 annually. Obviously this is not enough to live on, which is why so many musicians work at a second job.

Musicians who are able to come up with the "right" sound and make the right contacts in the industry may begin touring on a national level, increase their fan base, and sell recordings of their music. Those who are able to do this on a steady basis may have earnings in the $20,000 to $30,000 range. At the very top of the business, a few groups have earnings into the millions for one year. Even then, however, this money must be divided among the group members, backup singers, agents, and others.

Most pop and rock musicians are freelancers, moving from one performance to the next and getting paid by various clients. Because of this, they have no employer that provides benefits such as health insurance and paid vacation time. Therefore these musicians must provide their own benefits.

Work Environment

Creative people can be a temperamental bunch, and some musicians can be difficult to get along with. Working closely with such people can at times create a tense or unpleasant environment. On the other hand, the opportunity to perform with talented musicians can be inspiring and offer opportunities to learn new things about music. Rehearsing requires a great deal of time and late hours, but can result in excellent work. Pop and rock musicians may perform in dark, smoky bars, in large hotel dining rooms, or in open-air auditoriums. They must be prepared to work in a variety of settings, some of which may not have the best acoustics or the proper amount of space for all the instruments and band members. The professional musician learns to adapt to the performance area, making adjustments with sound systems, the music to be played, or even the instruments used. Travel is a part of this work. Even those musicians who only perform in one or two towns must get to and from different performance sites with their equipment in order to work. And any pop or rock musician who wants to advance his or her career should be prepared to be on the road a great deal of the time.

Outlook

There will always be thousands more rock and pop musicians than there are record contracts. But there will also always be opportunities for new performers with record companies and clubs. Record companies are always on the lookout for original sounds and talents. Even with a record deal, however, there are no guarantees of success. The music industry, and the CD-buying public, have fickle tastes. Often rock musicians are dropped by their label when record sales fail to meet expectations.

With recording studios becoming more sophisticated, artists can more effectively promote themselves with quality CDs. Record companies will be paying close attention to these independently produced CDs when scouting for new talent.

For More Information

For information on the music business and careers, contact:

American Federation of Musicians of the United States and Canada
1501 Broadway, Suite 600
New York, NY 10036
Tel: 212-869-1330
Email: info@afm.org
Web: http://www.afm.org

For information about the music field as well as career development opportunities, such as songwriting workshops for the pop music composer, contact:

American Society of Composers, Authors, and Publishers
One Lincoln Plaza
New York, NY 10023
Tel: 212-621-6000
Email: info@ascap.com
Web: http://www.ascap.com

Visit GigAmerica's Web site for helpful advice in the FAQ section as well as to learn about venues and other groups across the country.

GigAmercia
One Pennsylvania Plaza, Suite 2400
New York, NY 10119
Tel: 917-339-9012
Web: http://www.gigamerica.com

At select cities SGA offers song critiques and other workshops. Visit its Web site for more information.

Songwriters Guild of America (SGA)
National Projects Office
1560 Broadway, Suite 1306
New York, NY 10036
Tel: 212-768-7902
Web: http://www.songwriters.org

Screenwriters

English Theater/dance	School Subjects
Artistic Communication/ideas	Personal Skills
Primarily indoors Primarily one location	Work Environment
High school diploma	Minimum Education Level
$15,000 to $82,169 to $500,000+	Salary Range
None available	Certification or Licensing
Faster than the average	Outlook

Overview

Screenwriters write scripts for entertainment, education, training, sales, television, and films. They may choose themes themselves, or they may write on a theme assigned by a producer or director, sometimes adapting plays or novels into screenplays. Screenwriting is an art, a craft, and a business. It is a career that requires imagination and creativity, the ability to tell a story using both dialogue and pictures, and the ability to negotiate with producers and studio executives.

History

In 1894, Thomas Edison invented the kinetograph to take a series of pictures of actions staged specifically for the camera. In October of the same year, the first film opened at Hoyt's Theatre in New York. It was a series of acts performed by such characters as a strongman, a contortionist, and trained animals. Even in these earliest motion pictures, the plot or sequence of actions the film would portray was written down before filming began.

Newspaperman Roy McCardell was the first person to be hired for the specific job of writing for motion pictures. He wrote captions for photographs in an entertainment weekly. When he was employed by Biograph to write 10 scenarios, or stories, at $10 apiece, it caused a flood of newspapermen to try their hand at screenwriting.

The early films, which ran only about a minute and were photographs of interesting movement, grew into story films, which ran between 9 and 15 minutes. The demand for original plots led to the development of story departments at each of the motion picture companies in the period from 1910 to 1915. The story departments were responsible for writing the stories and also for reading and evaluating material that came from outside sources. Stories usually came from writers, but some were purchased from actors on the lot. The actor Genevieve (Gene) Gauntier, was paid $20 per reel of film for her first scenarios.

There was a continuing need for scripts because usually a studio bought a story one month, filmed the next, and released the film the month after. Some of the most popular stories in these early films were Wild West tales and comedies.

Longer story films began to use titles, and as motion pictures became longer and more sophisticated, so did the titles. In 1909-10, there was an average of 80 feet of title per 1,000 feet of film. By 1926, the average increased to 250 feet of title per 1,000 feet. The titles included dialogue, description, and historical background.

In 1920, the first Screen Writers Guild was established to ensure fair treatment of writers, and in 1927 the Academy of Motion Picture Arts and Sciences was formed, including a branch for writers. The first sound film, *The Jazz Singer,* was also produced in 1927. Screenwriting changed dramatically to adapt to the new technology.

From the 1950s to the 1980s, the studios gradually declined and more independent film companies and individuals were able to break into the motion picture industry. The television industry began to thrive in the 1950s, further increasing the number of opportunities for screenwriters. During the 1960s, people began to graduate from the first education programs developed specifically for screenwriting.

Today, most Americans have spent countless hours viewing programs on television and movie screens. Familiarity with these mediums has led many writers to attempt writing screenplays. This has created an intensely fierce marketplace with many more screenplays being rejected than accepted each year.

The Job

Screenwriters write dramas, comedies, soap operas, adventures, westerns, documentaries, newscasts, and training films. They may write original stories, or get inspiration from newspapers, magazines, or books. They may also write scripts for continuing television series. *Continuity writers* in broadcasting create station announcements, previews of coming shows, and advertising copy for local sponsors. Broadcasting scriptwriters usually work in a team, writing for a certain audience, to fill a certain time slot. Motion picture writers submit an original screenplay or adaptation of a book to a motion picture producer or studio. Playwrights submit their plays to drama companies for performance or try to get their work published in book form.

Screenwriters may work on a staff of writers and producers for a large company. Or they may work independently for smaller companies which hire only freelance production teams. Advertising agencies also hire writers, sometimes as staff, sometimes as freelancers.

Scripts are written in a two-column format, one column for dialogue and sound, the other for video instructions. One page of script equals about one minute of running time, though it varies. Each page has about 150 words and takes about 20 seconds to read. Screenwriters send a query letter outlining their idea before they submit a script to a production company. Then they send a standard release form and wait at least a month for a response. Studios buy many more scripts than are actually produced, and studios often will buy a script only with provisions that the original writer or another writer, will rewrite it to their specifications.

Requirements

High School

You can develop your writing skills in English, theater, speech, and journalism classes. Belonging to a debate team can also help you learn how to express your ideas within a specific time allotment and framework. History, government, and foreign language can contribute to a well-rounded education, necessary for creating intelligent scripts. A business course can be useful in understanding the complex nature of the film industry.

Postsecondary Training

There are no set educational requirements for screenwriters. A college degree is desirable, especially a liberal arts education which exposes you to a wide range of subjects. An undergraduate or graduate film program will likely include courses in screenwriting, film theory, and other subjects that will teach you about the film industry and its history. A creative writing program will involve you with workshops and seminars that will help you develop fiction writing skills.

Other Requirements

As a screenwriter, you must be able to create believable characters and develop a story. You must have technical skills, such as dialogue writing, creating plots, and doing research. In addition to creativity and originality, you also need an understanding of the marketplace for your work. You should be aware of what kinds of scripts are in demand by producers. Word processing skills are also helpful.

Exploring

One of the best ways to learn about screenwriting is to read and study scripts. It is advisable to watch a motion picture while simultaneously following the script. The scripts for such classic films as *Casablanca, Network,* and *Chinatown* are often taught in college screenwriting courses. You should read film-industry publications, such as *Daily Variety* (http://www.variety.com/), *Hollywood Reporter* (http://www.hollywoodreporter.com/), and *The Hollywood Scriptwriter* (http://www.hollywoodscriptwriter.com). There are a number of books about screenwriting, but they're often written by those outside of the industry. These books are best used primarily for learning about the format required for writing a screenplay. There are also computer software programs which assist with screenplay formatting.

The Sundance Institute, a Utah-based production company, accepts unsolicited scripts from those who have read the Institute's submission guidelines. Every January, they choose a few scripts and invite the writers to a five-day program of one-on-one sessions with professionals. The process is repeated in June, and also includes a videotaping of sections of chosen scripts. The Institute doesn't produce features, but they can often introduce writers to those who do. (See end of article for contact information.)

Most states offer grants for emerging and established screenwriters and other artists. Contact your state's art council for guidelines and application materials. In addition, several arts groups and associations hold annual contests for screenwriters. To find out more about screenwriting contests, consult a reference work such as *The Writer's Market*.

Students may try to get their work performed locally. A teacher may be able to help you submit your work to a local radio or television station or to a publisher of plays.

Employers

Most screenwriters work on a freelance basis, contracting with production companies for individual projects. Those who work for television may contract with a TV production company for a certain number of episodes or seasons.

Starting Out

The first step to getting a screenplay produced is to write a letter to the script editor of a production company describing yourself, your training, and your work. Ask if the editors would be interested in reading one of your scripts. You should also pursue a manager or agent by sending along a brief letter describing a project you're working on. A list of agents is available from the Writers Guild of America (WGA). If you receive an invitation to submit more, you'll then prepare a synopsis or treatment of the screenplay, which is usually from one to 10 pages. It should be in the form of a narrative short story, with little or no dialogue.

Whether you are a beginning or experienced screenwriter, it is best to have an agent, since studios, producers, and stars often return unsolicited manuscripts unopened to protect themselves from plagiarism charges. Agents provide access to studios and producers, interpret contracts, and negotiate deals.

It is wise to register your script ($10 for members, $22 for nonmembers) with the WGA. Although registration offers no legal protection, it is proof that on a specific date you came up with a particular idea, treatment, or script. You should also keep a detailed journal that lists the contacts you've made, the people who have read your script, etc.

Advancement

Competition is stiff among screenwriters, and a beginner will find it difficult to break into the field. More opportunities become available as a screenwriter gains experience and a reputation, but that is a process that can take many years. Rejection is a common occurrence in the field of screenwriting. Most successful screenwriters have had to send their screenplays to numerous production companies before they find one who likes their work.

Once they have sold some scripts, screenwriters may be able to join the WGA. Membership with the WGA guarantees the screenwriter a minimum wage for a production and other benefits such as arbitration. Some screenwriters, however, writing for minor productions, can have regular work and successful careers without WGA membership.

Those screenwriters who manage to break into the business can benefit greatly from recognition in the industry. In addition to creating their own scripts, some writers are also hired to "doctor" the scripts of others, using their expertise to revise scripts for production. If a film proves very successful, a screenwriter will be able to command higher payment, and will be able to work on high-profile productions. Some of the most talented screenwriters receive awards from the industry, most notably the Academy Award for best original or adapted screenplay.

Earnings

Wages for screenwriters are nearly impossible to track. Some screenwriters make hundreds of thousands of dollars from their scripts, while others write and film their own scripts without any payment at all, relying on backers and loans. Screenwriter Joe Eszterhas made entertainment news in the early 1990s when he received $3 million for each of his treatments for *Basic Instinct, Jade,* and *Showgirls.* In the early 2000s, many scripts by first-time screenwriters were sold for between $500,000 and $1 million. Typically, a writer will earn a percentage (approximately 1 percent) of the film's budget. Obviously, a lower budget film pays considerably less than a big production, starting at $15,000 or less. According to statistics compiled by the WGA-West, the median income for WGA-West members was $82,169 a year in 1998. Screenwriters who are WGA members also are eligible to receive health benefits.

Work Environment

Screenwriters who choose to freelance have the freedom to write when and where they choose. They must be persistent and patient; only one in 20 to 30 purchased or optioned screenplays is produced.

Screenwriters who work on the staff of a large company, for a television series, or under contract to a motion picture company, may share writing duties with others.

Screenwriters who do not live in Hollywood or New York will likely have to travel to attend script conferences. They may even have to relocate for several weeks while a project is in production. Busy periods before and during film production are followed by long periods of inactivity and solitude. This forces many screenwriters, especially those just getting started in the field, to work other jobs and pursue other careers while they develop their talent and craft.

Outlook

There is intense competition in the television and motion picture industries. There are currently over 11,000 members of the WGA. A 1999 report by the WGA found that only 53.8 percent of its members were actually employed the previous year. The report also focused on the opportunities for women and minority screenwriters. Despite employment for minority screenwriters substantially increasing, employment for women changed little in that decade. Eighty percent of those writing for feature films are white males. Though this domination in the industry will eventually change because of efforts by women and minority filmmakers, the change may be slow in coming. The success of independent cinema, which has introduced a number of women and minority filmmakers to the industry, will continue to contribute to this change.

As cable television expands and digital technology allows for more programming, new opportunities may emerge. Television networks continue to need new material and new episodes for long-running series. Studios are always looking for new angles on action, adventure, horror, and comedy, especially romantic comedy stories. The demand for new screenplays should increase slightly in the next decade, but the number of screenwriters is growing at a faster rate. Writers will continue to find opportunities in advertising agencies and educational and training video production houses.

For More Information

For guidelines on submitting a script for consideration for the Sundance Institute's screenwriting program, send a self-addressed stamped envelope or visit the following Web site:

Sundance Institute
8857 West Olympic Boulevard
Beverly Hills, CA, 90211
Email: la@sundance.org
Web: http://www.sundance.org

To learn more about the film industry, to read interviews and articles by noted screenwriters, and to find links to many other screenwriting-related sites on the Internet, visit the Web sites of the WGA:

Writers Guild of America
East Chapter
555 West 57th Street, Suite 1230
New York, NY 10019
Tel: 212-767-7800
Web: http://www.wgaeast.org

Writers Guild of America
West Chapter
7000 West Third Street
Los Angeles, CA 90048
Tel: 800-548-4532
Web: http://www.wga.org

Visit the following Web site to read useful articles on screenwriting:

Screenwriters Utopia
Web: http://www.screenwritersutopia.com

Singers

School Subjects	Music Speech
Personal Skills	Artistic Communication/ideas
Work Environment	Primarily indoors Primarily multiple locations
Minimum Education Level	High school diploma
Salary Range	$13,250 to $36,740 to $88,640+
Certification or Licensing	None available
Outlook	About as fast as the average

Overview

Singers perform opera, gospel, blues, rock, jazz, folk, classical, country, and other musical genres, before an audience or in recordings. Singers are musicians who use their voices as their instruments, and may perform as part of a band, choir, or other musical ensembles, or solo, whether with or without musical accompaniment. Singers, musicians, and related workers hold about 240,000 jobs in the United States.

History

"Song is man's sweetest joy," said a poet in the eighth century BC. Singers are those who use their voices as instruments of sound and are capable of relating music that touches the soul. The verb to sing is related to the Greek term omphe, which means "voice." In general, singing is related to music and thus to the Muses, the goddesses of ancient Greek religion who are said to watch over the arts and are sources of inspiration.

Singing, or vocal performance, is considered the mother of all music, which is thought of as an international language. In human history, before musical instruments were ever devised, there was always the voice, which has had the longest and most significant influence on the development of all musical forms and materials that have followed.

A precise, formal history of the singing profession is not feasible, for singing evolved in different parts of the world and in diverse ways at various times. A 40,000-year-old cave painting in France suggests the earliest evidence of music; the painting shows a man playing a musical bow and dancing behind several reindeer. Most civilizations have had legends suggesting that gods created song, and many myths suggest that nymphs have passed the art of singing to us. The Chinese philosopher Confucius (551-478 BC) considered music to be a significant aspect of a moral society, with its ability to portray emotions as diverse as joy and sorrow, anger and love.

There are certain differences between Eastern and Western music. In general, music of Middle Eastern civilizations has tended to be more complex in its melodies (although music from the Far East is often simplistic). Western music has been greatly influenced by the organized systems of musical scales of ancient Greece and has evolved through various eras, which were rich and enduring but can be defined in general terms. The first Western musical era is considered to have been the medieval period (c. 850-1450), when the earliest surviving songs were written by 12th-century French troubadours and German minnesingers; these poet-musicians sang of love, nature, and religion. The next periods include the Renaissance (c. 1450-1600), during which the musical attitude was one of calm and self-restraint; the Baroque (c. 1600-1750), a time of extravagance, excitement, and splendor; the Classical (c. 1750-1820), a return to simplicity; and the Romantic (c. 1820-1950), which represents a time of strong emotional expression and fascination with nature.

In primitive societies of the past and present, music has played more of a ritualistic, sacred role. In any case, singing has been considered an art form for thousands of years, powerfully influencing the evolution of societies. It is a large part of our leisure environment, our ceremonies, and our religions; the power of song has even been said to heal illness and sorrow. In antiquity, musicians tended to have more than one role, serving as composer, singer, and instrumentalist at the same time. They also tended to be found in the highest levels of society and to take part in events such as royal ceremonies, funerals, and processions.

The function of singing as an interpretive, entertaining activity was established relatively recently. Opera had its beginnings in the late 16th century in Italy and matured during the following centuries in other European countries. The rise of the professional singer (also referred to as the vocal virtuoso because of the expert talent involved) occurred in the 17th and 18th centuries. At this time, musical composers began to sing to wider audiences, who called for further expression and passion in singing.

Throughout the periods of Western music, the various aspects of song have changed along with general musical developments. Such aspects include melody, harmony, rhythm, tempo, dynamics, texture, and other characteristics. The structures of song are seemingly unlimited and have evolved from plainsong and madrigal, chanson and chorale, opera and cantata, folk and motet, anthem and drama, to today's expanse of pop, rock, country, rap, and so on. The development of radio, television, motion pictures, and various types of recordings (LP records, cassettes, compact discs, and digital audio) has had a great effect on the singing profession, creating smaller audiences for live performances yet larger and larger audiences for recorded music.

The Job

Essentially, singers are employed to perform music with their voices by using their knowledge of vocal sound and delivery, harmony, melody, and rhythm. They put their individual vocal styles into the songs they sing, and they interpret music accordingly. The inherent sounds of the voices in a performance play a significant part in how a song will affect an audience; this essential aspect of a singer's voice is known as its tone.

Classical singers are usually categorized according to the range and quality of their voices, beginning with the highest singing voice, the soprano, and ending with the lowest, the bass; voices in between include mezzo soprano, contralto, tenor, and baritone. Singers perform either alone (in which case they are referred to as soloists) or as members of an ensemble, or group. They sing by either following a score, which is the printed musical text, or by memorizing the material. Also, they may sing either with or without instrumental accompaniment. In opera (plays set to music), singers perform the various roles, much as actors, interpreting the drama with their voice to the accompaniment of a symphony orchestra.

Classical singers may perform a variety of musical styles, or specialize in a specific period; they may give recitals, or perform as members of an ensemble. Classical singers generally undergo years of voice training and instruction in musical theory. They develop their vocal technique, and learn how to project without harming their voices. Classical singers rarely use a microphone when they sing; nonetheless, their voices must be heard above the orchestra. Because classical singers often perform music from many different languages, they learn how to pronounce these languages, and often how to speak them as well. Those who are involved in opera work for opera companies in major cities throughout the country and often travel extensively. Some classical singers also perform in other musical areas.

Professional singers tend to perform in a certain chosen style of music, such as jazz, rock, or blues, among many others. Many singers pursue careers that will lead them to perform for coveted recording contracts, on concert tours, and for television and motion pictures. Others perform in rock, pop, country, gospel, or folk groups, singing in concert halls, nightclubs, and churches and at social gatherings and for small studio recordings. Whereas virtuosos, classical artists who are expertly skilled in their singing style, tend to perform traditional pieces that have been handed down through hundreds of years, singers in other areas often perform popular, current pieces, and often songs that they themselves have composed.

Another style of music in which formal training is often helpful is jazz. *Jazz singers* learn phrasing, breathing, and vocal techniques; often, the goal of a jazz singer is to become as much a part of the instrumentation as the piano, saxophone, trumpet, or trombone. Many jazz singers perform "scat" singing, in which the voice is used in an improvisational way much like any other instrument.

Folk singers perform songs that may be many years old, or they may write their own songs. Folk singers generally perform songs that express a certain cultural tradition; while some folk singers specialize in their own or another culture, others may sing songs from a great variety of cultural and musical traditions. In the United States, folk singing is particularly linked to the acoustic guitar, and many singers accompany themselves while singing.

A cappella singing, which is singing without musical accompaniment, takes many forms. A cappella music may be a part of classical music; it may also be a part of folk music, as in the singing of barbershop quartets. Another form, called doo-wop, is closely linked to rock and rhythm and blues music.

Gospel music, which evolved in the United States, is a form of sacred music; *gospel singers* generally sing as part of a choir, accompanied by an organ, or other musical instruments, but may also perform a cappella. Many popular singers began their careers as singers in church and gospel choirs before entering jazz, pop, blues, or rock.

Pop/rock singers (see the article "Pop/Rock Musicians") generally require no formal training whatsoever. Rock music is a very broad term encompassing many different styles of music, such as heavy metal, punk, rap, rhythm and blues, rockabilly, techno, and many others. Many popular rock singers cannot even sing. But rock singers learn to express themselves and their music, developing their own phrasing and vocal techniques. Rock singers usually sing as part of a band, or with a backing band to accompany them. Rock singers usually sing with microphones so that they can be heard above the amplified instruments around them.

All singers practice and rehearse their songs and music. Some singers read from music scores while performing; others perform from memory. Yet all must gain an intimate knowledge of their music, so that they can best convey its meanings and feelings to their audience. Singers must also exercise their voices even when not performing. Some singers perform as featured soloists and artists. Others perform as part of a choir, or as backup singers adding harmony to the lead singer's voice.

Requirements

High School

Many singers require no formal training in order to sing. However, those interested in becoming classical or jazz singers should begin learning and honing their talent when they are quite young. Vocal talent can be recognized in grade school students and even in younger children. In general, however, these early years are a time of vast development and growth in singing ability. Evident changes occur in boys' and girls' voices when they are around 12 to 14 years old, during which time their vocal cords go through a process of lengthening and thickening. Boys' voices tend to change much more so than girls' voices, although both genders should be provided with challenges that will help them achieve their talent goals. Young students should learn about breath control and why it is necessary; they should learn to follow a conductor, including the relationship between hand and baton motions and the dynamics of the music; and they should learn about musical concepts such as tone, melody, harmony, and rhythm.

During the last two years of high school, aspiring singers should have a good idea of what classification they are in, according to the range and quality of their voices: soprano, alto, contralto, tenor, baritone, or bass. These categories indicate the resonance of the voice; soprano being the highest and lightest, bass being the lowest and heaviest. Students should take part in voice classes, choirs, and ensembles. In addition, students should continue their studies in English, writing, social studies, foreign language, and other electives in music, theory, and performance.

There tend to be no formal educational requirements for those who wish to be singers. However, formal education is valuable, especially in younger years. Some students know early in their lives that they want to be singers and are ambitious enough to continue to practice and learn. These students are often advised to attend high schools that are specifically geared toward combined academic and intensive arts education in music, dance, and theater. Such schools can provide valuable preparation and guidance for those who plan to pursue professional careers in the arts. Admission is usually based on results from students' auditions as well as academic testing.

Postsecondary Training

Many find it worthwhile and fascinating to continue their study of music and voice in a liberal arts program at a college or university. Similarly, others attend schools of higher education that are focused specifically on music, such as the Juilliard School in New York. Such an intense program would include a multidisciplinary curriculum of composition and performance, as well as study and appreciation of the history, development, variety, and potential advances of music. In this type of program, a student would earn a bachelor of arts degree. To earn a bachelor of science degree in music, one would study musicology, which concerns the history, literature, and cultural background of music; the music industry, which will prepare one for not only singing but also marketing music and other business aspects; and professional performance. Specific music classes in a typical four-year liberal arts program would include such courses as introduction to music, music styles and structures, harmony, theory of music, elementary and advanced auditory training, music history, and individual instruction.

In addition to learning at schools, many singers are taught by private singing teachers and voice coaches, who help to develop and refine students' voices. Many aspiring singers take courses at continuing adult education centers, where they can take advantage of courses in beginning and advanced singing, basic vocal techniques, voice coaching, and vocal performance workshops. When one is involved in voice training, he or she must learn about good articulation and breath control, which are very important qualities for all singers. Performers must take care of their voices and keep their lungs in good condition. Voice training, whether as part of a college curriculum or in private study, is useful to many singers, not only for classical and opera singers, but also for jazz singers and for those interested in careers in musical theater. Many professional singers who have already "made it" continue to take voice lessons throughout their careers.

Other Requirements

In other areas of music, learning to sing and becoming a singer is often a matter of desire, practice, and an inborn love and talent for singing. Learning to play a musical instrument is often extremely helpful in learning to sing and to read and write music. Sometimes it is not even necessary to have a "good" singing voice. Many singers in rock music have less-than-perfect voices, and rap artists do not really sing at all. But these singers learn to use their voice in ways that nonetheless provides good expression to their songs, music, and ideas.

Exploring

Anyone who is interested in pursuing a career as a singer should obviously have a love for music. Listen to recordings as often as possible, and get an understanding of the types of music that you enjoy. Singing, alone or with family and friends, is one of the most natural ways to explore music and develop a sense of your own vocal style. Join music clubs at school, as well as the school band if it does vocal performances. In addition, take part in school drama productions that involve musical numbers.

Older students interested in classical music careers could contact trade associations such as the American Guild of Musical Artists, as well as read trade journals such as *Hot Line News* (published by Musicians National Hot Line Association), which covers news about singers and other types of musicians and their employment needs and opportunities. For information and news about very popular singers, read *Billboard* magazine (http://www.billboard.com), which can be purchased at many local bookshops and newsstands. Those who already know what type of music they wish to sing should audition for roles in community musical productions or contact trade groups that offer competitions. For example, the Central Opera Service (Metropolitan Opera, Lincoln Center, New York, NY 10023) can provide information on competitions, apprentice programs, and performances for young singers interested in opera.

There are many summer programs offered throughout the United States for high school students interested in singing and other performing arts. (See the end of article for contact information on these programs.) For example, Stanford University offers its Stanford Jazz Workshop each summer for students who are at least 12 years old. It offers activities in instrumental and vocal music, as well as recreation in swimming, tennis, and volleyball. For college students who are 18 years and older, the jazz workshop has a number of job positions available.

Another educational institute that presents a summer program is Boston University's Tanglewood Institute, which is geared especially toward very talented and ambitious students between the ages of 15 and 18. It offers sessions in chorus, musical productions, chamber music, classical music, ensemble, instrumental, and vocal practice. Arts and culture field trips are also planned. College students who are at least 20 years old can apply for available jobs at the summer Tanglewood programs. Students interested in other areas of singing can begin while still in high school, or even sooner. Many gospel singers, for example, start singing with their local church group at an early age. Many high school students form their own bands, playing rock, country, or jazz, and can gain experience performing before an audience, and even being paid to perform at school parties and other social functions.

Employers

There are many different environments in which singers can be employed, including local lounges, bars, cafes, radio and television, theater productions, cruise ships, resorts, hotels, casinos, large concert tours, and opera companies.

Many singers hire agents, who usually receive a percentage of the singer's earnings for finding them appropriate performance contracts. Others are employed primarily as studio singers, which means that they do not perform for live audiences but rather record their singing in studios for albums, radio, television, and motion pictures.

An important tactic for finding employment as a singer is to invest in a professional quality tape recording of your singing that you can send to prospective employers.

Starting Out

There is no single correct way of entering the singing profession. It is recommended that aspiring singers explore the avenues that interest them, continuing to apply and audition for whatever medium suits them. Singing is an extremely creative profession, and singers must learn to be creative and resourceful in the business matters of finding "gigs."

High school students should seek out any opportunities to perform, including choirs, school musical productions, and church functions. Singing teachers can arrange recitals and introduce students to their network of musician contacts.

Advancement

In the singing profession and the music industry in general, the nature of the business is such that singers can consider themselves to have "made it" when they get steady, full-time work. A measure of advancement is how well known and respected singers become in their field, which in turn influences their earnings. In most areas, particularly classical music, only the most talented and persistent singers make it to the top of their profession. In other areas, success may be largely a matter of luck and perseverance. A singer on Broadway, for example, may begin as a member of the chorus, and eventually become a featured singer. On the other hand, those who have a certain passion for their work and accept their career position tend to enjoy working in local performance centers, nightclubs, and other musical environments.

Also, many experienced singers who have had formal training will become voice teachers. Reputable schools such as Juilliard consider it a plus when a student can say that he or she has studied with a master.

Earnings

As with many occupations in the performing arts, earnings for singers are highly dependent on one's professional reputation and thus cover a wide range. To some degree, pay is also related to educational background (as it relates to how well one has been trained) and geographic location of performances. In certain situations, such as singing for audio recordings, pay is dependent on the number of minutes of finished music (for instance, an hour's pay will be given for each three and a half minutes of recorded song).

Singing is often considered a glamorous occupation. However, because it attracts so many professionals, competition for positions is very high. Only a small proportion of those who aspire to be singers achieve glamorous jobs and extremely lucrative contracts. Famous opera singers, for example earn $8,000 and more for each performance. Singers in an opera chorus earn between $600 and $800 per week. Classical soloists can receive between $2,000 and $3,000 per performance, while choristers may receive around $70 per performance. For rock singers, earnings can be far higher. Within the overall group of professional singers, studio and opera singers tend to earn salaries that are well respected in the industry; their opportunities for steady, long-term contracts tend to be better than for singers in other areas.

Average salaries for musicians, singers, and related workers were $36,740 in 2000, according to the *Occupational Outlook Handbook*. The lowest 10 percent earned less than $13,250 per year, while the highest 10 percent earned more than $88,640 annually.

Top earners in studio and opera earn an average of $70,000 per year, though some earn much more. Rock singers may begin by playing for drinks and meals only; if successful, they may earn tens of thousands of dollars for a single performance. Singers on cruise ships generally earn between $750 and $2,000 per week, although these figures can vary considerably. Also, many singers supplement their performance earnings by working at other positions, such as teaching at schools or giving private lessons or even working at jobs unrelated to singing. Median salaries for full-time elementary, middle, and secondary teachers in 2000 ranged from $37,610 to $42,080; full-time college professors earned an average of $58,400 in 1999-2000.

Because singers rarely work for a single employer, they generally receive no benefits, and must provide their own health insurance and retirement planning.

Work Environment

The environments in which singers work tend to vary greatly, depending on such factors as type of music involved and location of performance area. Professional singers often work in the evenings and during weekends, and many are frequently required to travel. Many singers who are involved in popular productions such as in opera, rock, and country music work in large cities such as New York, Las Vegas, Chicago, Los Angeles, and Nashville. Stamina and endurance are needed to keep up with the hours of rehearsals and performances, which can be long; work schedules are very often erratic, varying from job to job.

Many singers are members of trade unions, which represent them in matters such as wage scales and fair working conditions. Vocal performers who sing for studio recordings are represented by the American Federation of Television and Radio Artists; solo opera singers, solo concert singers, and choral singers are members of the American Guild of Musical Artists.

Outlook

Any employment forecast for singers will most probably emphasize one factor that plays an important role in the availability of jobs: competition. Because so many people pursue musical careers and because there tend to be no formal requirements for employment in this industry (the main qualification is talent), competition is most often very strong.

According to the U.S. Department of Labor, employment for singers, as for musicians in general, is expected to grow about as fast as the average for all other occupations through 2010. The entertainment industry is expected to grow during the next decade, which will create jobs for singers and other performers. Because of the nature of this work, positions tend to be temporary and part-time; in fact, of all members of the American Federation of Musicians, fewer than 2 percent work full-time in their singing careers. Thus, it is often advised that those who are intent on pursuing a singing career keep in mind the varied fields other than performance in which their interest in music can be beneficial, such as composition, education, broadcasting, therapy, and community arts management.

Those intent on pursuing singing careers in rock, jazz, and other popular forms should understand the keen competition they will face. There are thousands of singers all hoping to make it; only a very few actually succeed. However, there are many opportunities to perform in local cities and communities, and those with a genuine love of singing and performing should also possess a strong sense of commitment and dedication to their art.

For More Information

The following organizations have information on career opportunities, certification, and education resources:

American Federation of Musicians of the United States and Canada
1501 Broadway, Suite 600
New York, NY 10036
Tel: 212-869-1330
Web: http://www.afm.org

American Federation of Television and Radio Artists
260 Madison Avenue
New York, NY 10016-2402
Tel: 212-532-0800
Email: aftra@aftra.com
Web: http://www.aftra.org

Musicians National Hot Line Association
277 East 6100 South
Salt Lake City, UT 84107
Tel: 801-268-2000

National Association of Schools of Music
11250 Roger Bacon Drive, Suite 21
Reston, VA 20190
Tel: 703-437-0700
Email: info@arts-accredit.org
Web: http://www.arts-accredit.org/nasm

Opera America
1156 15th Street, Suite 810
Washington, DC 20005
Tel: 202-293-4466
Email: Frontdesk@operaamerica.org
Web: http://www.operaam.org

For information on music programs, contact the following:

Boston University, Tanglewood Institute
855 Commonwealth Avenue
Boston, MA 02215
Web: http://www.bu.edu/sfa/music/tanglewood

Stanford University, Jazz Workshop
Box 20454
Stanford, CA 94309
Tel: 650-736-0324
Email: info@stanfordjazz.org
Web: http://www.stanfordjazz.org

Songwriters

	School Subjects
English Music	

	Personal Skills
Artistic Communication/ideas	

	Work Environment
Primarily indoors Primarily one location	

	Minimum Education Level
High school diploma	

	Salary Range
$20,000 to $50,000 to $1,000,000+	

	Certification or Licensing
None available	

	Outlook
About as fast as the average	

Overview

Songwriters write the words and music for songs, including songs for recordings, advertising jingles, and theatrical performances. We hear the work of songwriters every day, and yet most songwriters remain anonymous, even if a song's performer is famous. Many songwriters perform their own songs.

History

Songwriting played an important part in the growth of the United States. The early pioneers wrote songs as a way to relax. Some of the difficult experiences of traveling, fighting over land, farming, and hunting for food were put into words by early songwriters, and the words set to music, for the guitar, banjo, piano, and other instruments. Francis Scott Key (1780?-1843) became famous for writing the words to the "Star Spangled Banner," set to a popular drinking tune.

Toward the end of the 19th century, sheet music was sold by dozens and even hundreds of publishing companies, centered in New York City in what became known as Tin Pan Alley. This name was coined by a songwriter and journalist named Monroe Rosenfeld, referring to the sounds of many voices and pianos coming from the open windows of the street where many of the music publishers were located. By the 1880s, sheet music sold in the millions; most songs were introduced on the stages of musical theater, vaudeville, and burlesque shows. Radio became an important medium for introducing new songs in the 1920s, followed by the introduction of sound movies in the 1930s. Sheet music became less important as musical recordings were introduced. This presented difficulties for the songwriter and publisher, because the sales of sheet music were easier to control. In the 1940s, the first associations for protecting the rights of the songwriters and publishers were formed; among the benefits songwriters received were royalties for each time a song they had written was recorded, performed, or played on the radio or in film.

By the 1950s, Tin Pan Alley no longer referred to a specific area in New York but was used nationwide to denote popular songs in general, and especially a type of simple melody and sentimental and often silly lyric that dominated the pop music industry. The rise of rock and roll music in the 1950s put an end to Tin Pan Alley's dominance. Many performers began to write their own songs, a trend that became particularly important in the 1960s. In the late 1970s, a new type of songwriting emerged. Rap music, featuring words chanted over a musical background, seemed to bring songwriting full circle, back to the oral traditions of its origins.

The Job

There are many different ways to write a song. A song may begin with a few words (the lyric) or with a few notes of a melody, or a song may be suggested by an idea, theme, or product. A song may come about in a flash of inspiration or may be developed slowly over a long period of time. Songwriters may work alone, or as part of a team, in which one person concentrates on the lyrics while another person concentrates on the music. Sometimes there may be several people working on the same song.

"One of the most important things," says songwriter Beth McBride, "is collecting your ideas, even if they're only fragments of ideas, and writing them down. Sometimes a song comes to me from beginning to end, but I can't always rely on inspiration." McBride performed with the band "B and the Hot Notes," for which she wrote and recorded original music. She currently fronts a musical duo called "Acoustisaurus Rex" and is involved in another recording project. "A lot of my writing has been personal, derived from experience. Also from the observation of others' experiences."

Most popular songs require words, or lyrics, and some songwriters may concentrate on writing the words to a song. These songwriters are called *lyricists*. Events, experiences, or emotions may inspire a lyricist to write lyrics. A lyricist may also be contracted to write the words for a jingle, a musical, or adapt the words from an existing song for another project.

Some songwriters do no more than write the words to a potential song, and leave it to others to develop a melody and musical accompaniment for the words. They may sell the words to a music publisher, or work in a team to create a finished song from the lyric. Some lyricists specialize in writing the words for advertising jingles. They are usually employed by advertising agencies and may work on several different products at once, often under pressure of a deadline.

In songwriting teams, one member may be a lyricist, while the other member is a composer. The development of a song can be a highly collaborative process. The composer might suggest topics for the song to the lyricist; the lyricist might suggest a melody to the composer. Other times, the composer plays a musical piece for the lyricist, and the lyricist tries to create lyrics to fit with that piece.

Composers for popular music generally have a strong background in music, and often in performing music as well. They must have an understanding of many musical styles, so that they can develop the music that will fit a project's needs. Composers work with a variety of musical and electronic equipment, including computers, to produce and record their music. They develop the different parts for the different musical instruments needed to play the song. They also work with musicians who will play and record the song, and the composer conducts or otherwise directs the musicians as the song is played.

Songwriters, composers, and musicians often make use of MIDI (musical instrument digital interface) technology to produce sounds through synthesizers, drum machines, and samplers. These sounds are usually controlled by a computer, and the composer or songwriter can mix, alter, and refine the sounds using mixing boards and computer software. Like analog or acoustic instruments, which produce sounds as a string or reed or drum head vibrates with air, MIDI creates digital "vibrations" that can produce sounds similar to acoustic instruments or highly unusual sounds invented by the songwriter. Synthesizers and other sound-producing machines may each have their own keyboard or playing mechanism, or be linked through one or more keyboards. They may also be controlled through the computer, or with other types of controls, such as a guitar controller, which plays like a guitar, or foot controls. Songs can be stored in the computer, or transferred to tape or compact disc.

Many, if not most, songwriters combine both the work of a lyricist and the work of a composer. Often, a songwriter will perform his or her own songs as well, whether as a singer, a member of a band, or both. Playing guitar has helped McBride in the writing of lyrics and music. "My songwriting has become more sophisticated as my playing has become more sophisticated," she says.

For most songwriters, writing a song is only the first part of their job. After a song is written, songwriters usually produce a "demo" of the song, so that the client or potential purchaser of the song can hear how it sounds. Songwriters contract with recording studios, studio musicians, and recording engineers to produce a version of the song. The songwriter then submits the song to a publishing house, record company, recording artist, film studio, or others, who will then decide if the song is appropriate for their needs. Often, a songwriter will produce several versions of a song, or submit several different songs for a particular project. There is always a chance that one, some, or all of their songs will be rejected.

Requirements

High School

You should take courses in music that involve you with singing, playing instruments, and studying the history of music. Theater and speech classes will help you to understand the nature of performing, as well as involve you in writing dramatic pieces. You should study poetry in an English class, and try your hand at composing poetry in different forms. Language skills can also be honed in foreign-language classes and by working on student literary magazines. An understanding of how people act and think can influence you as a lyricist, so take courses in psychology and sociology.

Postsecondary Training

There are no real requirements for entering the field of songwriting. All songwriters, however, will benefit from musical training, including musical theory and musical notation. Learning to play one or more instruments, such as the piano or guitar, will be especially helpful in writing songs. Not all songwriters need to be able to sing, but this is helpful.

Songwriting is an extremely competitive field. Despite a lack of formal educational requirements, prospective songwriters are encouraged to continue their education through high school and preferably towards a college degree. Much of the musical training a songwriter needs, however, can also be learned informally. In general, you should have a background in music theory, and in arrangement and orchestration for multiple instruments. You should be able to read music, and be able to write it in the proper musical notation. You should have a good sense of the sounds each type of musical instrument produces, alone and in combination. Understanding harmony is important, as well as a proficiency in or understanding of a variety of styles of music. For example, you should know what makes rock different from reggae, blues, or jazz. Studies in music history will also help develop this understanding.

On the technical side, you should understand the various features, capabilities, and requirements of modern recording techniques. You should be familiar with MIDI and computer technology, as these play important roles in composing, playing, and recording music today.

There are several organizations that help lyricists, songwriters, and composers. The National Academy of Songwriters offers weekly song evaluation workshops in California. The Nashville Songwriters Association offers workshops, seminars, and other services, as well as giving annual awards to songwriters. The Songwriters and Lyricists Club in New York provides contacts for songwriters with music-business professionals. These, and other organizations, offer songwriting workshops and other training seminars.

Other Requirements

Many elements of songwriting cannot really be learned but are a matter of inborn talent. A creative imagination and the ability to invent melodies and combine melodies into a song are essential parts of a songwriting career. As you become more familiar with your own talents, and with songwriting, you'll learn to develop and enhance your creative skills.

"I enjoy observing," Beth McBride says. "I also enjoy the challenge of finding the most succinct way of saying something and making it poetic. I enjoy the process of finding that perfect turn of phrase. I really love language and words."

Exploring

The simplest way to gain experience in songwriting is to learn to play a musical instrument, especially the piano or guitar, and to invent your own songs. Joining a rock group is a way to gain experience writing music for several musicians. Most schools and communities have orchestras, bands, and choruses that are open to performers. Working on a student-written musical show is ideal training for the future songwriter.

If you have your own computer, think about investing in software, a keyboard, and other devices that will allow you to experiment with sounds, recording, and writing and composing your own songs. While much of this equipment is highly expensive, there are plenty of affordable keyboards, drum machines, and software available today. Your school's music department may also have such equipment available.

Employers

Most songwriters work freelance, competing for contracts to write songs for a particular artist, television show, video program, or for contracts with musical publishers and advertising agencies. They will meet with clients to determine the nature of the project and to get an idea of what kind of music the client seeks, the budget for the project, the time in which the project is expected to be completed, and in what form the work is to be submitted. Many songwriters work under contract with one or more music publishing houses. Usually, they must fulfill a certain quota of new songs each year. These songwriters receive a salary, called an advance or draw, that is often paid by the week. Once a song has been published, the money earned by the song goes to pay back the songwriter's draw. A percentage of the money earned by the song over and above the amount of the draw goes to the songwriter as a royalty. Other songwriters are employed by so-called "jingle houses," that is, companies that supply music for advertising commercials. Whereas most songwriters work in their own homes or offices, these songwriters work at the jingle house's offices. Film, television, and video production studios may also employ songwriters on their staff.

Starting Out

Songwriting is a very competitive career and difficult to break into for a beginner. The number of high-paying projects is limited. Often, beginning songwriters start their careers writing music for themselves or as part of a musical group. They may also offer their services to student films, student and local theater productions, church groups, and other religious and non-profit organizations, often for free or for a low fee.

Many songwriters get their start while performing their own music in clubs and other places; they may be approached by a music publisher, who contracts them for a number of songs. Other songwriters record demos of their songs and try to interest record companies and music publishers. Some songwriters organize showcase performances, renting a local club or hall and inviting music industry people to hear their work. Songwriters may have to approach many companies and publishers before they find one willing to buy their songs. A great deal of making a success in songwriting is in developing contacts with people active in the music industry.

Some songwriters get their start in one of the few entry-level positions available. Songwriters aspiring to become composers for film and television can find work as orchestrators or copyists in film houses. Other songwriters may find work for music agents and publishers, which will give them an understanding of the industry and increase their contacts in the industry, as they develop their songwriting skills. Those interested in specializing in advertising jingles may find entry level work as music production assistants with a jingle house. At first, such jobs may involve making coffee, doing paperwork, and completing other clerical tasks. As you gain more exposure to the process of creating music, you may begin in basic areas of music production, or assist experienced songwriters.

Advancement

It is important for a songwriter to develop a strong portfolio of work and a reputation for professionalism. Songwriters who establish a reputation for the quality of their work will receive larger and higher-paying projects as their careers proceed. They may be contracted to score major motion pictures, or to write songs for major recording artists. Ultimately, they may be able to support themselves on their songwriting alone and also have the ability to pick and choose the projects they will work on.

In order to continue to grow with the music industry, songwriters must be tuned into new musical styles and trends. They must also keep up with developments in music technology. A great deal of time is spent making and maintaining contacts with others in the music industry.

Songwriters specializing in jingles and other commercial products may eventually start up their own jingle house. Other songwriters, especially those who have written a number of hit songs, may themselves become recording artists.

For many songwriters, however, success and advancement is a very personal process. A confidence in your own talent will help you to create better work. "I'm not as vulnerable about my work," Beth McBride says. "And I want to open up my subject matter, to expand and experiment more."

Earnings

Songwriters' earnings vary widely, from next to nothing to many millions of dollars. A beginning songwriter may work for free, or for low pay, just to gain experience. A songwriter may sell a jingle to an advertising agency for $1,000 or may receive many thousands of dollars if his or her work is well-known. Royalties from a song may reach $20,000 per year or more per song, and a successful songwriter may earn $100,000 or more per year from the royalties of several songs. A songwriter's earnings may come from a combination of royalties earned on songs and fees earned from commercial projects.

Those starting as assistants in music production companies or jingle houses may earn as little as $20,000 per year. Experienced songwriters at these companies may earn $50,000 per year or more.

Because most songwriters are freelance, they will have to provide their own health insurance, life insurance, and pension plans. They are usually paid per project, and therefore receive no overtime pay. When facing a deadline, they may have to work many more hours than eight hours a day or 40 hours a week. Also, songwriters are generally responsible for recording their own demos and must pay for recording studio time, studio musicians, and production expenses.

Work Environment

Songwriters generally possess a strong love for music, and regardless of the level of their success, usually find fulfillment in their careers because they are doing what they love to do. As freelancers, they will control how they spend their day. They will work out of their own home or office. They will have their own instruments, and possibly their own recording equipment as well. Songwriters may also work in recording studios, where conditions can vary, from noisy and busy, to relaxed and quiet.

Writing music can be stressful. When facing a deadline, songwriters may experience a great deal of pressure while trying to get their music just right and on time. They may face a great deal of rejection before they find someone willing to publish or record their songs. Rejection remains a part of the songwriter's life, even after success.

Many songwriters work many years with limited or no success. On the other hand, songwriters experience the joys of creativity, which has its own rewards.

Outlook

Most songwriters are unable to support themselves from their songwriting alone and must hold other part-time or full-time jobs while writing songs in their spare time. The competition in this industry is extremely intense, and there are many more songwriters than paying projects. This situation is expected to continue into the next decade.

There are a few bright spots for songwriters. The recent rise of independent filmmaking has created more venues for songwriters to compose film scores. Cable television also provides more opportunities for song writing, both in the increased number of advertisements and in the growing trend for cable networks to develop their own original programs. Many computer games and software feature songs and music, and this area should grow rapidly in the next decade. Another boom area is the World Wide Web. As more and more companies, organizations, and individuals set up multimedia Web sites, there will be an increased demand for songwriters to create songs and music for these sites. Songwriters with MIDI capability will be in the strongest position to benefit from the growth created by computer uses of music. In another field, legalized gambling has spread to many states in the country, a large number of resorts and theme parks have opened, and as these venues produce their own musical theater and shows, they will require more songwriters.

Success in songwriting is a combination of hard work, industry connections, and good luck. The number of hit songs is very small compared to the number of songwriters trying to write them.

For More Information

For membership information, contact:

American Society of Composers, Authors, and Publishers
One Lincoln Plaza
New York, NY 10023
Tel: 800-952-7227
Email: info@ascap.com
Web: http://www.ascap.com

Visit the Songwriter's section of the BMI Web site to learn more about performing rights, music publishing, copyright, and the business of songwriting.

Broadcast Music Inc. (BMI)
320 West 57th Street
New York, NY 10019-3790
Tel: 212-586-2000
Email: newyork@bmi.com
Web: http://www.bmi.com

To learn about the young composer's competition and other contests, contact:

National Association of Composers, USA
PO Box 49256, Barrington Station
Los Angeles, CA 90049
Tel: 310-541-8213
Email: nacusa@music-usa.org
Web: http://www.music-usa.org/nacusa

For membership information, contact:

Songwriters Guild of America
1222 16th Avenue South, Suite 25
Nashville, TN 37212
Web: http://www.songwriters.org

Stage Production Workers

Mathematics Theater/dance	School Subjects
Artistic Technical/scientific	Personal Skills
Primarily indoors One location with some travel	Work Environment
High school diploma Apprenticeship	Minimum Education Level
$15,000 to $27,000 to $36,000	Salary Range
None available	Certification or Licensing
About as fast as the average	Outlook

Overview

Stage production workers handle the behind-the-scenes tasks that are necessary for putting on theatrical performances. Their responsibilities include costume and set design, installing lights, rigging, sound equipment, and scenery, and set building for events in parks, stadiums, arenas, and other places. During a performance they control the lighting, sound, and various other aspects of a production that add to its impact on an audience. These technicians work in close cooperation with the stage director, lighting director, actors, and various prop people. In addition, they work directly with theater shops in the construction of sets. Others are involved in the management of the theater or production. Theatre Communications Group reports that in a late 1990s survey of the industry, there were approximately 10,000 technical workers employed by nearly 200 participating nonprofit theatres.

History

Theatrical performance is among the most ancient of human art forms. Primitive societies wore masks and costumes during ritual ceremonies designed to ward off evil spirits and to promote the welfare of the society.

Greek theater also included masks and costumes. As Greek theater developed, its costumes also became more elaborate and were used to emphasize characters' status within the world of the play. Greek theater was originally performed in a large circle, and the scenery was minimal; around 460 BC a wood skene, or stage structure, was added to the back of the circle through which the actors could enter or exit the circle. Painted scenery was attached to the skene; special effects included cranes for flying actors over the stage. As theater became more professional, people began to specialize in the different areas of theater, such as controlling the scenery, directing the action, and creating the costumes. An important development in early theater was the addition of the raised stage.

By the time of the Romans, theaters were freestanding structures that could be covered and hold large audiences. Scenery was often mounted on three-sided prismlike structures that could be rotated to change the scenery during a performance. Medieval performances were often extremely elaborate. Performances were generally held outdoors, and sometimes on wagon stages that moved through a town during the performance. Special effects were often spectacular, with flames and smoke, flood, realistic massacres complete with flowing blood, hangings, crucifixions, and the like.

Nonreligious theater rose into prominence during the 16th century. The first dedicated theater was build in 1576 in London, followed by many other theaters, including the famous Globe Theater where the work of William Shakespeare (1564-1616) was performed. Costumes, primarily representing contemporary dress, were often highly elaborate and quite costly.

The Renaissance and the rediscovery of Greek and Roman theater brought scenery back into prominence in the theater. The development of perspective techniques in painting and drawing led to more realistic settings as backdrops for the performance. More methods were developed for changing the scenery during the performance, although these scene changes continued to be made in front of the audience. Flying machines and other special effects were added; and, as theater moved indoors, stages were lighted by candles and oil lamps.

Many of the features of present-day theater evolved during the 17th and 18th centuries. A new profession emerged, that of stage designer. One of the most influential of these designers was Giacomo Torelli (1608-78), who invented a mechanical system for raising and lowering settings. Earlier settings, however, were not generally designed for a specific performance, and costumes were not often historically accurate. By the end of the 18th century, stage direction, which had generally been given by the playwright or by one of the leading actors, became a more recognized part of preparing a theatrical performance.

Lighting and scenery developed rapidly in the 19th century. Gas lamps replaced candles and oil lamps, and innovations such as the limelight (a stage light consisting of an oxyhydrogen flame directed on a cylinder of lime and usually equipped with a lens to concentrate the light in a beam) and the spotlight were introduced. Stages began to feature trap doors, and scenery could be raised from below the stage or lowered from above the stage. Many theaters incorporated hydraulic lifts to raise and lower scenery, props, and actors through the trap doors. The look of a theater production, in its costumes, settings, and props, became at once more realistic and more historically accurate. Settings became increasingly more elaborate, and the introduction of panoramas gave motion effects to the stage. Special effects could include the use of real animals on stage, volcanic eruptions, sinking ships, and storms complete with wind and rain. During this period, it became more common that a play would remain in the same theater through many performances. These elaborately planned and staged productions required dedicated directors to oversee the entire production. Another innovation of the 19th century was the use of a curtain to hide the stage during scene changes.

The art of stage production changed considerably with the introduction of electricity to theaters at the end of the 19th century. It became possible to use lighting effects as a major interpretive element in stage productions. Stage machinery became more elaborate, even to the point of moving a whole stage, so that sets could be transformed in new ways. In the 20th century, recording and amplification techniques introduced a wider range of musical and sound effects than ever before. These changes added new dimensions to the tasks of stagehands and other workers.

The Job

For small productions with fewer employees, stage workers must be able to do a variety of tasks. In larger productions (such as those on Broadway), responsibilities are divided among many different workers, each with a special area of expertise. The following paragraphs describe some of these areas of responsibility:

Stage technicians include many different workers, such as carpenters, prop makers, lighting designers, lighting-equipment operators, sound technicians, electricians, riggers, and costume workers.

When installing stage equipment, stage technicians begin with blueprints, diagrams, and specifications concerning the stage area. They confer with the stage manager to establish what kinds of sets, scenery, props, lighting, and sound equipment are required for the event or show, and where each should be placed.

Then the technicians gather props provided by the production company and build other props or scenery using hammers, saws, and other hand tools and power tools. If they are working in a theater, they climb ladders or scaffolding to the gridwork at the ceiling and use cables to attach curtains, scenery, and other equipment that needs to be moved, raised, and lowered during performances. They may need to balance on and crawl along beams near the ceiling to connect the cables.

Stage technicians also position lights and sound equipment on or around the stage. They clamp light fixtures to supports and connect electrical wiring from the fixtures to power sources and control panels.

The sound equipment used on and around stages usually includes microphones, speakers, and amplifiers. Technicians position this equipment and attach the wires that connect it to power sources and to the sound-mixing equipment that controls the volume and quality of the sound.

During rehearsals and performances, stage technicians in some theaters may follow cues and pull cables that raise and lower curtains and other equipment. Sometimes they also operate the lighting and sound equipment.

Costume designers choose the costumes necessary for a production, including their style, fabric, color, and pattern. They may do research to design clothes that are historically and stylistically authentic. They discuss their ideas with the stage director and make sketches of costumes for the director's approval. They check stores and specialty clothing shops for garments that would meet their needs. If appropriate items are not found, designers may have the costumes made from scratch. They oversee the purchasing of fabric and supervise the workers who actually create the costumes. Costume designers also work with actors to make sure that costumes fit properly. In a large production, they may supervise several assistants who help in all aspects of the job, including locating hard-to-find items.

Other workers help to complete the desired appearance of the performers. *Hairstylists* and *makeup artists* use cosmetics, greasepaint, wigs, plastics, latex, and other materials to change the look of their hair and skin. Once costumes have been made for a show, *wardrobe supervisors* keep them in good condition for each performance by ironing, mending, and cleaning them, and doing any necessary minor alterations. *Dressers* help performers to get dressed before a show and change quickly between scenes.

Requirements

High School

Requirements vary for different kinds of stage production workers and technicians. In general, a high school diploma is necessary and a college degree is highly recommended. High school students interested in careers in theatrical production should take college-preparatory courses such as English, history, and mathematics. In addition, they should take drama courses and participate in school theatrical performances in a variety of ways, such as acting or working on sets to helping with promotion.

Postsecondary Training

People who want to work in technical fields such as lighting and sound design would benefit by taking courses in history and art, as well as subjects such as electricity, electronics, computers, mathematics, and physics. Craft workers such as carpenters and electricians do not need a college degree, and they often learn their work skills through apprenticeships. Makeup artists need to study anatomy and art subjects like sculpture and portrait painting. Costume designers ought to have a graduate degree in design or fine arts, as well as a well-developed artistic sense.

Certification or Licensing

Many stage production workers belong to unions. Union membership may be required to get a job, although requirements vary in different areas and even in different theaters in the same city. For example, various theater workers belong to the United Scenic Artists or the International Alliance of Theatrical Stage Employees. Some unions require members to pass a competency test before they can begin work. Prospective stage production workers need to investigate union requirements, if any, that apply in their field of interest in their local area.

Other Requirements

Passion for theatre as an art form is essential to bear with the long hours and often low pay associated with these professions. The ability to get along well with others is also important, since stage technicians often work in teams. Patience and flexibility will be needed as directors and designers may change their minds about set plans or demand a stage, lighting effect, or costume piece that might seem difficult or challenging creatively as well as financially.

Exploring

If you are interested in a stage production career, you can learn a great deal by becoming involved in high school theatrical performances. If possible, try to gain experience in many different capacities, including acting, stage design, lighting, and special effects. Another way to get experience is by working as a volunteer for amateur community theater productions or special benefit events. With this sort of broad experience, you may be able to get a paid or volunteer summer job assisting in a professional theater.

Experiences gained in other fields may be helpful background for some stage production jobs. For example, aspiring costume designers can learn by working for clothes designers in a fashion-oriented business.

Employers

Stage production workers and technicians may be employed by theatre, dance, music, and other performing arts companies. They more often receive full-time employment from those companies that have their own facilities, although companies that tour year-round often need to keep technical workers on staff. In addition, managers of performing arts facilities, such as theaters, opera houses, arenas, or auditoriums, may hire full-time technicians. Often, technical workers are not hired by a single employer; many find work with different companies and/or facility managers on a freelance basis.

Starting Out

Competition is very keen for nearly all positions associated with theatrical productions, so you should get as much experience and become as versatile a worker as possible. It is often necessary to begin working on a volunteer basis or start in a position unrelated to your desired field. Because of the great difficulty in securing satisfying jobs, many people who want to work in stage production end up in other professions.

Job seekers should not be discouraged by the tight labor market. In New York, Chicago, and Los Angeles, publications specifically about local activities in the theater and television industries are an excellent source of information that may lead to jobs. In many cities, local newspapers regularly list production plans for area community theater groups. Sometimes college internships in theater jobs or recommendations from drama teachers can lead to permanent employment.

Advancement

Advancement opportunities vary according to the type of work performed. Often, workers advance by moving to different theaters where they handle greater responsibilities associated with more complicated productions. Those who develop good reputations in the industry may be sought out by other employers to do similar jobs in new settings.

Costume designers can work on larger theatrical productions or for television production companies. Alternatively, they may establish independent consulting firms and work for a variety of clients.

Competition for the best positions is so strong that many workers remain in the same job and consider salary increases as evidence of their success.

Earnings

Earnings vary widely according to the worker's experience, job responsibilities, the geographic location of the theater, and the budget of the performance. In addition, the International Alliance of Theatrical Stage Employees reports that different local chapters have different pay scales, although its members, who are mostly employed at the largest commercial houses and on Broadway, generally earn more than nonmembers.

According to a member survey by Theatre Communications Group, Inc. (TCG), a beginning carpenter earned $15,000 annually in the late 1990s. Scene shop supervisors averaged $27,000 per year, while production managers averaged $36,000. Stage managers had a median salary of $31,000 per year. Set and lighting designers generally work on a freelance basis and are paid widely varying fees on a per-project basis.

The pay of costume designers is often based on the number of costumes designed. Experienced designers working in major markets such as New York and Chicago earn more than those in other markets. Local unions often determine salary scales. Some costume designers working in summer theaters earn around $500 or more a week, but others may earn substantially less. TCG reports that costume shop managers earned average salaries of $30,000 in the late 1990s.

Most full-time workers receive health insurance and other benefits, as established by the local union contract. Because workers are hired for a particular time period, vacations are rarely provided.

Work Environment

Working conditions in theaters vary from the lavish in a few theaters to small, simply equipped facilities in many community theaters. Many theaters are hot and stuffy during performances, or drafty and cold when empty. Stage production workers can expect to work long hours and spend much time on their feet. Many work evenings and weekends. People who work behind the scenes in theaters must be concerned about safety. Those who work with lights and electric cables risk burns, while those who climb rigging or scaffolding need to use care to avoid falls.

Costume designers work in design shops sketching and designing costumes, in theaters fitting performers, and in libraries and other locations researching costume possibilities. They spend long hours preparing for a show, with most of their work done before and during the rehearsal period.

Outlook

Present employment patterns for workers in this field are probably a good guide to the situation for the foreseeable future. According to Theatre Communications Group, the industry is remaining steady; there are few new theaters appearing that can pay living wages for stage production workers and technicians, but those that have existed are healthy and surviving. Today, theaters tend to be concentrated in large metropolitan areas, so the number of job possibilities is greatest there, but so too is the competition for those jobs. Many stage workers start out instead with small theatrical groups. After they develop skills and a local reputation, they may be able to move to bigger, better-paying markets. They may have to work part-time, do volunteer work in amateur theater, or support themselves in unrelated fields for extended periods while waiting for better theater jobs.

In the late 1990s, theater groups came under increasing financial pressures; public funding for the arts in general is tight. As a result, many smaller theaters are finding it difficult to survive. Productions, even among the larger theaters, are likely to become less elaborate to lower operating costs. These factors could limit the need for new stage production employees. However, theater remains a popular form of entertainment and an important cultural resource. Those who are skilled in a variety of production areas stand the best chance of employment. For example, someone who knows about both lighting and sound systems, or both set design and props, is more likely to get a desirable position in theater.

For More Information

For information on salaries, insurance, and educational programs, contact:

International Alliance of Theatrical Stage Employees, Moving Picture Technicians, Artists and Allied Crafts of the United States and Canada
1430 Broadway, 20th Floor
New York, NY 10018
Tel: 212-730-1770
Web: http://www.iatse.lm.com

For information on educational programs, surveys, and careers, contact:

Theater Communications Group
355 Lexington Avenue, 4th floor
New York, NY 10017
Tel: 212-697-5230
Email: tcg@tcg.org
Web: http://www.tcg.org

Stunt Performers

Overview

Stunt performers, also called *stuntmen* and *stuntwomen,* are actors who perform dangerous scenes in motion pictures. They may fall off tall buildings, get knocked from horses and motorcycles, imitate fist fights, and drive in high-speed car chases. They must know how to set up "stunts" that are both safe to perform and believable to audiences. In these dangerous scenes, stunt performers are often asked to double, or take the place, of a star actor.

History

There have been stunt performers since the early years of motion pictures. Frank Hanaway, believed to be the first stunt performer, began his career in the 1903 film *The Great Train Robbery.* A former U.S. cavalryman, Hanaway had developed the skill of falling off a horse unharmed. Until the introduction of sound films in the 1920s, stunt performers were used mostly in slapstick comedy films, which relied on "sight-gags" to entertain the audience.

The first stuntwoman in motion pictures was Helen Gibson, who began her stunt career in the 1914 film series *The Hazards of Helen*. Chosen for the job because of her experience performing tricks on horseback, Gibson went from doubling for Helen Holmes, the star actress, to eventually playing the lead role herself. Among her stunts was jumping from a fast-moving motor-cycle onto an adjacent moving locomotive.

Despite the success of Helen Gibson, most stunt performers were men. For dangerous scenes, actresses were usually doubled by a stuntman wear-ing a wig and the character's costume. Because films usually showed stunts at a distance, audiences could not tell the switch had been made.

Discrimination in the film industry also resulted in few minorities work-ing as stunt performers. White men doubled for American Indians, Asians, Mexicans, and African-Americans by applying makeup or other material to their skin. This practice was called painting down.

As the motion picture industry grew, so did the importance of stunt per-formers. Because injury to a star actor could end a film project and incur a considerable financial loss for the studio, producers would allow only stunt performers to handle dangerous scenes. Even so, star actors would com-monly brag that they had performed their own stunts. Only a few, such as Helen Gibson and Richard Talmadge, actually did.

Beginning in the 1950s the growth in the number of independent, or self-employed, producers brought new opportunities for stunt performers. In general, independent producers were not familiar with stunt work and came to rely on experienced stunt performers to set up stunt scenes and to find qualified individuals to perform them. Stunt performers who did this kind of organizational work came to be called stunt coordinators.

The Stuntmen's Association, the first professional organization in the field, was founded in 1960. Its goal was to share knowledge of stunt tech-niques and safety practices, to work out special problems concerning stunt performers, and to help producers find qualified stunt performers. Other organizations followed, including the International Stunt Association, the Stuntwomen's Association, the United Stuntwomen's Association, Stunts Unlimited, and Drivers Inc. As a result of these organizations, stunt per-formers are now better educated and trained in stunt techniques.

An increasing number of women and minorities have become stunt per-formers since the 1970s. The Screen Actors Guild (SAG), the union that rep-resents stunt performers, has been at the vanguard of this change. In the 1970s SAG banned the practice of painting down, thus forcing producers to find, for example, an African-American stuntman to double for an African-American actor. SAG also began to require that producers make an effort to find female stunt performers to double for actresses. Only after showing that a number of qualified stuntwomen have declined the role can a producer hire a stuntman to do the job.

Over the years, new technology has changed the field of stunt work. Air bags, for example, make stunts safer, and faster cars and better brakes have given stunt performers more control. Stunt performers, however, still rely on their athletic ability and sense of timing when doing a dangerous stunt.

The Job

Stunt performers work on a wide variety of scenes which have the potential for causing serious injury, including car crashes and chases; fist and sword fights; falls from cars, motorcycles, horses, and buildings; airplane and helicopter gags; rides through river rapids; and confrontations with animals, such as in a buffalo stampede. Although they are hired as actors, they rarely perform a speaking role. Some stunt performers specialize in one type of stunt.

There are two general types of stunt roles: double and nondescript. The first requires a stunt performer to "double"—to take the place of—a star actor in a dangerous scene. As a double, the stunt performer must portray the character in the same way as the star actor. A nondescript role does not involve replacing another person and is usually an incidental character in a dangerous scene. An example of a nondescript role is a driver in a freeway chase scene.

The idea for a stunt usually begins with the screenwriter. Stunts can make a movie not only exciting but also profitable. Action films, in fact, make up the majority of box-office hits. The stunts, however, must make sense within the context of the film's story.

Once the stunts are written into the script, it is the job of the director to decide how they will appear on the screen. Directors, especially of large, action-filled movies, often seek the help of a stunt coordinator. *Stunt coordinators* are individuals who have years of experience performing or coordinating stunts and who know the stunt performer community well. A stunt coordinator can quickly determine if a stunt is feasible and, if so, what is the best and safest way to perform it. The stunt coordinator plans the stunt, oversees the setup and construction of special sets and materials, and either hires or recommends the most qualified stunt performer. Some stunt coordinators also take over the direction of action scenes. Because of this responsibility, many stunt coordinators are members not only of the Screen Actors Guild but of the Directors Guild of America.

Although a stunt may last only a few seconds on film, preparations for the stunt can take several hours or even days. Stunt performers work with such departments as props, makeup, wardrobe, and set design. They also work closely with the special effects team to resolve technical problems and ensure safety. The director and the stunt performer must agree on a camera angle that will maximize the effect of the stunt. These preparations can save a considerable amount of production time and money. A carefully planned stunt can often be completed in just one take. More typically, the stunt person will have to perform the stunt several times until the director is satisfied with the performance.

Stunt performers do not have a death wish. They are dedicated professionals who take great precautions to ensure their safety. Air bags, body pads, or cables might be used in a stunt involving a fall or a crash. If a stunt performer must enter a burning building, special fire-proof clothing is worn and protective cream is applied to the skin. Stunt performers commonly design and build their own protective equipment.

Stunt performers are not only actors but also athletes. Thus, they spend much of their time keeping their bodies in top physical shape and practicing their stunts.

Requirements

High School

Take physical education, dance, and other courses that will involve you in exercise, weight-lifting, and coordination. Sports teams can help you develop the athletic skills needed. In a theater class, you'll learn to take direction, and you may have the opportunity to perform for an audience.

Postsecondary Training

There is no minimum educational requirement for becoming a stunt performer. Most learn their skills by working for years under an experienced stunt performer. A number of stunt schools, however, do exist, including the United Stuntmen's Association National Stunt Training School. You can also benefit from enrolling in theater classes.

Among the skills that must be learned are specific stunt techniques, such as how to throw a punch; the design and building of safety equipment; and production techniques, such as camera angles and film editing. The more a stunt performer knows about all aspects of filmmaking, the better that person can design effective and safe stunts.

Certification or Licensing

There is no certification available, but, like all actors, stunt performers working in film and TV must belong to the Screen Actors Guild (SAG). Many stunt performers also belong to the American Federation of Television and Radio Artists (AFTRA). As a member of a union, you'll receive special benefits, such as better pay and compensation for overtime and holidays.

Other Requirements

Stunt work requires excellent athletic ability. Many stunt performers were high school and college athletes, and some were Olympic or world champions. Qualities developed through sports such as self-discipline, coordination, common sense, and coolness under stress are essential to becoming a successful stunt performer. As a stunt performer, you must exercise regularly to stay in shape and maintain good health. You should also have some understanding of the mechanics of the stunts you'll be performing—you may be working with ropes, cables, and other equipment.

Because much of the work involves being a stunt double for a star actor, it is helpful to have a common body type. Exceptionally tall or short people, for example, may have difficulty finding roles.

Exploring

There are few means of gaining experience as a stunt performer prior to actual employment. Involvement in high school or college athletics is helpful, as is acting experience in a school or local theater. As an intern or extra for a film production, you may have the opportunity to see stunt people at work. Theme parks and circuses also make much use of stunt performers; some of these places allow visitors to meet the performers after shows.

Employers

Most stunt performers work on a freelance basis, contracting with individual productions on a project-by-project basis. Stunt performers working on TV projects may have long-term commitments if serving as a stand-in for a regular character. Some stunt performers also work in other aspects of the entertainment industry, taking jobs with theme parks, and live stage shows and events.

Starting Out

Most stunt performers enter the field by contacting stunt coordinators and asking for work. Coordinators and stunt associations can be located in trade publications. To be of interest to coordinators, you'll need to promote any special skills you have, such as stunt driving, skiing, and diving. Many stunt performers also have agents who locate work for them, but an agent can be very difficult to get if you've had no stunt experience. If you live in New York or Los Angeles, you should volunteer to work as an intern for an action film; you may have the chance to meet some of the stunt performers, and make connections with crew members and other industry professionals. You can also submit a resume to the various online services, such as StuntNET (http://www.stuntnet.com), that are used by coordinators and casting directors. If you attend a stunt school, you may develop important contacts in the field.

Advancement

New stunt performers generally start with simple roles, such as being one of 40 people in a brawl scene. With greater experience and training, stunt performers can get more complicated roles. Some stunt associations have facilities where stunt performers work out and practice their skills. After a great deal of experience, you may be invited to join a professional association such as the Stuntmen's Association of Motion Pictures, which will allow you to network with others in the industry.

About five to 10 years of experience are usually necessary to become a stunt coordinator. Some stunt coordinators eventually work as a director of action scenes.

Earnings

The earnings of stunt performers vary considerably by their experience and the difficulty of the stunts they perform. In 2002, the minimum daily salary of any member of the Screen Actors Guild (SAG), including stunt performers, was $655. A stunt coordinator working in motion pictures earned a daily minimum wage of $1,008, and a weekly minimum of $3,979. Stunt coordinators who work in television productions earn a daily minimum wage of $655, and a weekly minimum of $2,440. Though this may seem like a lot of money, few stunt performers work every day. According to the SAG, the majority of its 90,000 members make less than $7,500. But those who are in high demand can receive salaries of well over $100,000 a year.

Stunt performers usually negotiate their salaries with the stunt coordinator. In general, they are paid per stunt; if they have to repeat the stunt three times before the director likes the scene, the stunt performer gets paid three times. If footage of a stunt is used in another film, the performer is paid again. The more elaborate and dangerous the stunt, the more money the stunt performer receives. Stunt performers are also compensated for overtime and travel expenses. Stunt coordinators negotiate their salaries with the producer.

Work Environment

The working conditions of a stunt performer change from project to project. It could be a studio set, a river, or an airplane thousands of feet above the ground. Like all actors, they are given their own dressing rooms.

Careers in stunt work tend to be short. The small number of jobs is one reason, as are age and injury. Even with the emphasis on safety, injuries commonly occur, often because of mechanical failure, problems with animals, or human error. The possibility of death is always present. Despite these drawbacks, a large number of people are attracted to the work because of the thrill, the competitive challenge, and the chance to work in motion pictures.

Outlook

There are over 2,500 stunt performers who belong to the SAG, but only a fraction of those can afford to devote themselves to film work full time. Stunt coordinators will continue to hire only very experienced professionals, making it difficult to break into the business.

The future of the profession may be affected by computer technology. In more cases, filmmakers may choose to use special effects and computer-generated imagery for action sequences. Not only can computer effects allow for more ambitious images, but they're also safer. Safety on film sets has always been a serious concern; despite innovations in filming techniques, stunts remain very dangerous. However, using live stunt performers can give a scene more authenticity, so talented stunt performers will always be in demand.

For More Information

Visit the SAG Web site to read the online stunt performer's guide and So You Wanna Be an Actor.

Screen Actors Guild (SAG)
5757 Wilshire Boulevard
Los Angeles, CA 90036-3600
Tel: 323-954-1600
Email: saginfo@sag.org
Web: http://www.sag.com

For information about the USA training program, contact:

United Stuntmen's Association (USA)
2723 Saratoga Lane
Everett, WA 98203
Tel: 425-290-9957
Email: bushman4@prodigy.net
Web: http://www.stuntschool.com

Index